Naked Eye-Opener
To Reach the Dream
You Must Forget About It

Copyright © 2015 by Gisela Hausmann

Updated: Copyright © September 2019

ISBN 978-0-9963893-6-5 (paperback)
ISBN 978-0-9963893-7-2 (ebook)

Library of Congress Control Number:2019915375

* * *

Educ-Easy Books
POB 6366
Greenville, SC 29606
www.GiselaHausmann.com

Quantity Sales. For details please contact the address above.

Book Design: Gisela Hausmann
Editor: Divya Lavanya M.

Copyright acknowledgements:
Kateryna Fedorova Art (three doodle style vector illustrations)
Rat007 (Potala Palace in Night Time, Lhasa, Tibet)
Danny Xu (Mt. Everest at Sunset)
By SunPhotography (All planets of Solar System. Illustration)
Gisela Hausmann (historic pictures of Lhasa & and Kashmir 87/88)

*

Some names have been changed to protect the privacy of others.

Thank You!

*

A HUGE thank you to my fans,
who appreciate my "naked books"
thereby pushing for a world with less fluff;

*

my children, Anna and George,
who support me in everything I do;

*

and my editor, Divya Lavanya M.,
who puts up with my delivering manuscripts late, again and again;

*

Onward and Upwards!
To Your Success!

*

*

*Why does the eye see a thing more clearly in dreams
than the imagination when awake?*
— Leonardo da Vinci

*

A man is not old until his regrets take the place of his dreams.
— Yiddish proverb

*

*If I tell you my dream, you might forget it.
If I act on my dream, perhaps you will remember it,
but if I involve you, it becomes your dream too.*
— Tibetan Proverb

*

Dear Reader,

Writing this book has been a dream come true because I deeply believe in sharing knowledge how *all of us* can get ahead. As it often is with dreams it was a two-step process.

I began investigating the topic in 2001, the year after my husband died. Before tragedy struck I was on a roll, working hard and by all accounts living the life of my dreams. Afterwards, for about a decade, just about any dream became an elusive prey.

That's when I figured out that "working harder than you ever thought you could" and "having the right mindset" just isn't enough. The type of successes we achieve at any given time massively influence what next goals we can reach, unless – we move "in an express lane" to the zone where dreams can be achieved easier.

When I published my "Naked Eye-Opener" in 2017 readers recognized it as a different kind of self-help book, one that offered a realistic path rather than the usual suggestions. Still, then I was unable to offer a path how practically everybody can achieve "their dream." The time isn't always right to offer a "best bet" that fits every man, woman, and teenager with different interests and talents, all over the world.

Relatively recently, three events caused an "express lane to the zone where dreams can be achieved easier" to open up. And so I updated the "Naked Eye-Opener" which now lies before you. I promise you entertaining stories you have never heard before as well as eye-opening revelations.

Enjoy,

Gisela

CONTENT

INTRODUCTION

If you have read any number of self-help books, you have probably come to the conclusion that even though there is no shortage of advice on "how to reach your dream," it is not easy to achieve the *specific* success for which you are looking.

The most commonly presented success formulas are:

- Decide what you want!
- Don't try to be like Everybody Else!
- Work harder than you ever thought you could!
- Focus!
- Believe in yourself!
- Hold Yourself Accountable!

But, that's not all. There are also

- Just say "Yes"!
- Just say "No"!
- Reject Rejection!
- Dream Big!
- Live your dream and share your passions!

And many more...

Worldwide, millions of people try to do all of the above every day. Some end up with questions like

- "Focus? On what?... It's not working."
- "When should I say 'Yes' or say 'No'?"
- "I am trying so hard NOT to be like everybody else. Why am I doing worse than everybody else?"

Though media reports and social media postings make it appear as if it has never been easier to reach the dream and become insanely successful, too many budding entrepreneurs learn that much of the buzz is hyped, fake, or can't be independently verified.

And what's with the people who want to "help" others to reach their dreams? If they really are self-made millionaires who live in amazing estates, why do they charge others hundreds or even thousands of dollars for sharing their methods that don't offer a real success guarantee? And how come these people's stories are always rags-to-riches stories?

Still, there is no denying that the Age of the Internet created unbelievable opportunities for thousands of people, from homemakers who amass tens of thousands of followers by sharing their day-to-day stories to artists who become overnight successes to billionaires Jeff Bezos and Jack Ma, who reign the e-commerce arena. What's their secret? How did they manage to make their dreams come true, or were they maybe not dreaming at all?

~*~

And who am I that I believe I can offer insights to this topic?

THE NOBODY EVERYBODY WANTS TO BE

I am a "nobody" like the "nobody everybody wants to be." I don't live in a huge mansion but in a 1,000-square-foot old bungalow from the sixties, in the woods. Wild bunnies hop through my backyard, and at night, I can hear owls hoot in the trees that surround my house. Still, the next shopping center with a good hundred stores, restaurants, and even a movie theater is only a five-minute drive away.

I renovated this house myself. My girlfriends think it is the cutest house they have ever seen. Due to the cleverly selected location and the deliberately planned renovations, I hardly ever have to run my air conditioner. In the summer, my electricity bill is still only about $80 per month. I also have a well on my property and therefore don't have to pay for water. My life is not burdened by overhead costs. Because my house is on a small mountain, the air is clean; I can admire the stars every night.

When I come home, no butler takes my coat. Instead, my eyes fall on my *not-working* but decorative fireplace, which I remodeled myself.

Naturally, I am proud that I managed to turn this outdated feature into a refined focal point – with my own hands. I **am invested** in my dream home through the exhausting search it took to find this house (I looked at 126 houses), money, and my own handy work.

Before I had children, I traveled thousands of miles through forty-seven countries – the cheap way! I slept in youth hostels where I shared rooms with strangers, on benches in airports, in train stations, and even in a lifeboat once or twice.

Amazingly, though nobody ever rolled out a red carpet for me anywhere, I got an opportunity to meditate in the Dalai Lama's former bedroom at the Potala Palace in Lhasa, Tibet, alone, by myself, for half an hour. I have also taken a picture of former President Gorbachev from up-close, at the Kremlin in Moscow. The KGB agents, who caught me getting that close to the president, let me go. Among other experiences, I have trekked through the Kashmir Valley, ridden on an elephant in Jaipur, India, and on a camel in the Mongolian desert. I have also done target shooting with friends on a Sicilian beach and gambled in Las Vegas and Macao.

Still, my life is not all milk and honey. My husband died when I was only thirty-eight years old. As if this wasn't tragic enough, my baby brother, my best friend since my teenage years, and one of my two aunts died the following four years. There were many months when I was afraid to pick up the phone. Because all my relatives live in Europe, I had to raise my two children alone, literally alone. Especially during the Great Recession, I went through an unbelievable amount of stress and despair. Still, I did not compromise and came out stronger.

These days I write books that make many people happy.

And, I read a lot.

Indeed, I read thousands of books including self-help books, and that's how one day I realized that at least the many self-help books I read were missing the essential detail that made everything I just described possible.

Here is the simple answer to all questions about SUCCESS:

Success comes from being invested! Before we can apply any of the previously mentioned success formulas, we have to be invested – the right way.

Please note, I am not speaking about making financial investments but about giving our all to what we believe in, laboriously, emotionally, and earnestly.

"Being invested" means having ownership; it is not about money but about advancing what we believe in. "Being invested" is also about finding happiness in what we do because positive feelings encourage creativity and open new doors.

Here is the craziest story about "being invested" I ever heard, personally.

THE CRATE

In college, I took two courses with Austria's legendary Professor Hans Hass, diving pioneer and author of thirty-something books. Though he would have rejected the term, people called him the Austrian Jacques Cousteau. Then already in his mid-sixties, Hass read about his "Energon Theory." Many students took this course because they saw it an opportunity to hear from a man who was considered a legend. Hass was the first man to swim with sharks.

The extremely popular author was a gifted storyteller who occasionally entertained his students with stories from his life. One time he told us how the research materials for his thesis almost got destroyed during WWII. It was probably a fitting story for students, or at least so I saw it then.

During World War II, Hass had been working at the Stazione Zoologica in Naples, Italy, studying Bryozoa, which are aquatic, invertebrate animals. During that time, British Royal Air Force bombarded the city of Naples frequently, because it was home to the Port of Naples as well as many rail, industrial, and petroleum facilities, all of which were strategic targets. At some point, war action began to heat up to the point that Hass decided to leave the city.

Trying to return to Berlin, home of his future Alma Mater, he had his most valuable possession, a crate with samples of Bryozoa, loaded into the cargo car. Shortly before the train was supposed to leave the station, Hass was still standing on the platform and watching over the cargo car. Suddenly, the air sirens went off. Hass could hear bombs falling somewhere. People began to get hysterical and shouted loud commands in Italian. Everybody started running even though no bombs were falling on the station's compound or anywhere close. This behavior surprised Hass, because in Naples, hearing air sirens was not unusual. Hass stopped one of the frantic people and asked why everybody was panicking.

The frightened man only pointed at the train standing next to Hass' passenger train. It was a special cargo train with petroleum cars. The people ran because they knew if the British bombers managed to hit only one car of the petroleum train, the whole train station could blow up.

Though the situation was life threatening, Hass decided to save his crate with the samples of Bryozoa. [I know you are raising your eyebrows right now. When I heard the story first, I did too.] Hass, a tall, strong man and also a trained decathlon athlete, tried to open the cargo car, but it was locked. As he examined the car, he saw that it had a window, which was protected by metal bars.

There was only one other person in the station who wasn't running; it was a young boy. Hass asked the boy, who just seemed to wait for him, if he wanted to help, and the boy said yes. Then, Hass made the impossible happen. With his bare hands, he bent apart the metal bars which protected the window, far enough so the boy could climb through.

At this point of the story Hass remarked something like, "Though I did not know where I took the strength from, the thought that I could lose everything I worked for gave me super human strength."

The boy was able to find the crate. Then Hass lifted the crate and the boy back onto the platform, and under the hail of flying glass pieces, the two of them ran for cover while carrying the crate. Bombs began falling on the station's compound. Minutes later, the train got hit, but Hass, the boy, and the crate were already safe. A few months later, Hass graduated from the University of Berlin "summa cum laude" with highest honor.

Naturally, I thought that he was a dedicated, totally crazy scientist, who wanted to tell a moral story to illustrate how important it is to be dedicated to your research work. Or something like that.

Another student asked Hass, if he wasn't scared. Hass replied that he did not have time to think about that. If the crate was lost, not only would he not graduate, considering how the war was going, he might not get a chance to work in the Mediterranean region again.

WHAT DO WE SAVE?

Probably, you and I would not have saved the samples of Bryozoa, because you and I aren't and will never be invested into the research of Bryozoa. To us, they are aquatic invertebrate animals with a funky Latin name. We would have run, like the other people.

As unusual as this story sounds, it isn't. Whereas the Austrian diving pioneer Hass was concerned about losing his crate with samples of Bryozoa, the American media mogul Ted Turner once said that he was more scared of losing a sailing race than of dying.

Ted Turner, a world-class sailor, participated as the owner and skipper of his yacht "Tenacious" in the famous Fastnet Race, 1979, off the coasts of South England and Ireland. On the second day of the race, a large depression, known as "low Y," began to form. It created the most treacherous conditions with maximum winds of Force 10 on the Beaufort scale; the lowest recorded pressure was 979 hPa. To save the sailors who participated in this race, the largest ever rescue operation in peace-time was put in motion. Of the 303 starters, only 86, not even a third of the participants, finished. There were 194 retirements and 24 abandonments; and, sadly, fifteen sailors died.

And, Ted Turner?

He won this infamous race. In his book *"Call me Ted,"* he wrote that he was more scared of losing the race than of dying.

While Hass was invested in his studies, Turner was invested in winning races. Turner had already won every important sailing race, including the America Cup 1977, but not the Fastnet Race. Since the Fastnet Race is held only every two years, not even this terrible storm could stop him from trying to win.

Disregarding life-threatening danger in favor of pursuing a goal is not a male domain. It is not even reserved for adults.

Amelia Earhart was invested in flying. Among her achievements are "First woman to fly the Atlantic solo" (1932), "First person to fly the Atlantic twice" (1932), "First woman to fly nonstop, coast-to-coast across the U.S." (1933), and many more. Sadly, Earhart disappeared or perished on her 1937 world flight while attempting to set a new record.

In 2009, at the age of sixteen, Australian sailor Jessica Watson became the youngest person to complete a southern hemisphere solo circumnavigation, a trip that lasted from October 18, 2009 to May 15, 2010. Jessica is the same age as my own daughter. I cannot even imagine how I would feel about my daughter sailing alone by herself for six months around the globe.

Still, even though it might appear that the ability to ignore life-threatening danger has something to do with success, it is really the quality of "being invested" that gives us the strength to succeed.

Almost all of us would jump into a swollen river to save our own child in danger of drowning, or even anybody's child. Every day we read about ordinary people taking heroic actions and achieving the ultimate success of saving somebody's life.

Almost all of us are invested in life, love, and friendship.

WE ARE ALWAYS INVESTED – SOMEHOW

Naturally, being invested in life, love, friendship or a business idea doesn't have to be dangerous.

One of the most famous stories of "being invested" is Thomas Alva Edison's light bulb story. Even elementary students get to hear this story about not-giving-up, and that Edison did not give up because he was invested in finding out how to build a working light bulb.

> *"I have not failed. I've just found 10,000 ways that won't work."* – Thomas A. Edison

At this point, you may be thinking, "But I don't even want to be as successful as Edison. I'd be happy if I could find my dream job, buy my dream home, buy a college fund for my children, put some money aside and take a dream vacation every year, or even only every other year."

We think that because listening to the stories of Earhart, Turner, and Edison it appears that we have to be immensely invested to achieve success.

To clarify this matter is the subject of this book.

One of the truths the self-help industry hardly ever mentions is that all of us "are invested in something" every day, whether we see it or not. Humans cannot help but get invested.

Don't believe that? Here's the proof.

How often have you heard somebody say, "Getting fired (or laid-off) was the best thing that ever happened to me"?

As soon as we begin working somewhere, most of us become invested **beyond** working for our paycheck. Surely you too have a few friends who claim to hate their employers, yet, instead of looking for a new job or learning a new skill, they focus only on what the company they can't stand should do to increase revenue or achieve some other goal. That's because they are invested in their role in their company.

My friend Dennis knows the exact number of days he has to work until he can retire from his "ridiculously underpaid" job, yet he keeps working unpaid overtime because he knows "what's expected from him." [Notice that Dennis' verbatim statement is passive voice.] Even though he can't wait until he doesn't "have to walk through these doors ever again," a few times per week Dennis voluntarily gives more than he is getting paid for, and that too quite lousily.

Though I encouraged him to apply at other companies, he won't, and the only way his situation would change is if his company would fire him or lay him off, which they won't, for obvious reasons.

Steve Jobs may be the most famous person who publicly recognized that "getting fired from Apple" was one of the best things that ever happened to him. In fact, it helped him in entering one of the most creative periods in his life. Had he not left Apple in 1985, Jobs probably would have wasted a lot of time butting heads with Apple's board. Leaving the company freed him to focus on his love for computers, and so he founded NEXT, and then purchased Pixar, and moved on to revolutionize six industries.

Other people get laid off and follow a completely new path because they finally get a chance to reinvent themselves in the industry they want to be invested in and are not held back by previous investments.

Here is what I have not found in any of the books I read:
1) Humans are always successful with whatever they **want** to do.
2) Humans always **apply** the success formulas.

HOWEVER:

We succeed according to what we are invested in. The trick to achieving the specific success we are looking for lies in carefully selecting what we want to be invested in.

~*~

The following story tells an example all of us can relate to much better than having to ponder whether we should risk our lives to save a crate or win a race, or not.

TWO TOTALLY DIFFERENT KINDS OF INVESTMENTS FROM A to Z

This is the story of two indie authors who were looking for book reviews. Today, an author's success is measured, in part, by the number of online reviews their work receives.

Both authors, let's call them **Andy** and **Zack**, had discovered my award-winning book "Naked Truths About Getting Book Reviews." The book explains how to contact Amazon top reviewers properly to increase the chances that they accept an indie author's book for review. Both, Andy and Zack, had purchased my book but reacted completely differently.

1. Within two days, Andy tweeted, "Sent 90+ emails to Amazon reviewers in US & UK overnight. So far 10 positives!!! Think I love you!"

2. Within two days Zack emailed me, "... Lately, I've had many problems with 'reviewers' who request an e-book from me but then never deliver on the review. My only comfort is that maybe someday they will read the e-book and be entertained. Maybe I'm too timid, but I won't send another e-mail to remind them of their 'obligation.' They have to live with themselves..."

It is easy to see how Andy acted decisively because he felt "being invested" in his work, and rightfully so. Writing a book is a considerable investment, especially when it comes to time. Writing a book can take years.

Contrary to Andy, Zack does not appear to be invested enough to risk sending out request emails. But indeed, Zack too was heavily invested.

Let's see how.

A

Andy was so invested in his book that he plowed through the list of 10,000 Amazon top reviewers in only two days.

Coming from **his state of "being invested,"** Andy applied the success formulas

- **Decide what you want!**

[Andy wanted book reviews regardless of what it would take.]

- **Have a Vision!**

[Naturally, I don't know how many reviews Andy wanted to get, but he did not stop working after writing half-a-dozen emails. He wrote more than ninety emails.]

- **Focus!**

[Andy was focused. He combed through the entire list in only two days.]

- **Work harder than you ever thought you could!**

[He did that too. I have never even heard of an author who worked through the entire list of 10,000 reviewer profiles in only two days.]

- **Believe in yourself!**

[He not only believed in himself but also in his book.]

- **Reject Rejection!**

[I believe that during these two days Andy rejected even the idea that his requests could be denied. He acted out of his deep-rooted belief "My book is great, and every top reviewer wants to read it."]

- **Live your dream and share your passions!**

[Four weeks later, Andy's book had accumulated 10 new book reviews (including reviews from five Amazon Top reviewers #1,000 or better).]

Z

Here is Zack's e-mail again.

"... Lately, I've had many problems with 'reviewers' who request an e-book from me but then never deliver on the review. My *only comfort* is that maybe someday they will read the e-book and be entertained. Maybe I'm too timid, but I won't send another e-mail to remind them of their 'obligation.' They have to live with themselves..."

Zack **was invested in his pain** over various reviewers' failure to review his book.

The fact that one or more reviewers didn't review a book they requested is not uncommon. Every author can tell stories about this topic. But, instead of reminding the reviewers, contacting different reviewers, or even exploring if he should re-edit his book, Zack elected to sulk.

I believe Zack was just as much **invested in his disappointments** as Andy was invested in his belief that his book could get the best reviews. Zack too applied the same success formulas as Andy did.

- **Decide what you want!**

[Zack wanted to learn about every method for getting book reviews.]

- **Have a Vision!**

[Zack had a vision of *evil* book reviewers, who would "have to live with the fact that they did not live up to their obligations..."]

- **Focus!**

[Zack was focused on finding confirmation that there is no magical, miraculous way of receiving guaranteed free book reviews.]

- **Work harder than you ever thought you could!**

[Zack invested in a new book which he read immediately even though he had known that he probably would not do whatever the book presented.]

- **Believe in yourself!**

[Zack believed and probably *still* believes that he is a victim.]

- **Reject Rejection!**

[Zack rejected my book's rejection of his claim that there are no reviewers who want to review his book. He was too invested in his feeling sorry for himself to even consider trying a new method.]

- **Live your dream and share your passions!**

[Zack's dream was to indulge in "his only comfort" that maybe *someday* the reviewers he contacted will read his book. And, he passionately shared that he was a victim and that reviewers just did not live up to their obligations.]

Conclusion

Both authors, Andy and Zack, achieved "success" by building on their state of being invested.

Both of them applied the same success formulas though in the end they achieved totally different outcomes due to the fact that they were invested in different ways.

Did you notice how Zack "shifted his dream" of becoming a bestselling author to indulging in the feeling that his book was an underappreciated, unrecognized gem?

Zack applied the success formulas so he could still "claim success." That's why he did not want to contact even only five book reviewers, just as an experiment. If only one of the five book reviewers would have replied, "Sure, send your book right now. I am free right now," this one reply would have forced Zack to reevaluate his entire state of being invested.

*

As humans, we cannot help "getting and being invested." At any given moment, all of us are invested somehow. Even if we lie on a sofa watching the football game, though we know that we should do this or that, we are invested in our own comfort.

Sometimes **we tweak our application of the success formulas so we can prove the success** and don't have to figure out how we could reach our dream goal.

So, what's the real problem?

Why are some people capable of applying the success formulas in a way that is more beneficial to reach their *specific dream*?

THE REAL PROBLEM IS TODAY'S USAGE OF THE WORD "DREAM"

The dictionary defines

dream

    noun, \\'drēm\\
(1): an idea or vision that is created in your imagination and that is not real
(2): something that you have wanted very much to do, be, or have for a long time

***

While I am not sure when exactly it happened, a few decades ago the word "dream" became an integral part of marketing. That led to some kind of confusion on how we are supposed to try to achieve success.

Every day we read

- Will you be living the life of your dreams?
- How to Buy Your Dream Home!
- How to Land Your Dream Job in ...x... number of Steps
- Catapult yourself toward the life you've always dreamed of!
- Bring your dreams to life – now!

And similar slogans...

People who manage to be hired for their dream jobs, who buy their dream houses, and who take dream vacations are considered to be more successful than people who work a job, live in a decent house, and go camping. Society has adopted a view of what a dream job is, what a dream house looks like (e.g., it features stainless steel appliances), and how dream vacations feel.

In other words, marketers and maybe our society itself reduced the definition of the word "dream" to "something that you have wanted very much to do, be, or have" and dropped the other definition – "an idea or vision that is created in your imagination and that is not real."

Reading sponsored postings on social media sites, it almost seems as if "the dream" is something everybody can and should achieve and that "reaching the dream" is a state of waiting, like being pregnant. Therefore, thousands of people and organizations "want to help us to reach our dreams." Usually, they also want to charge big bucks for this help.

Noticing all of that, I decided to look for a different kind of definition of "the dream."

*

As a mass media specialist, I studied **pictures** my entire life. Therefore I searched for the word "dream" on Google Images. My search would show me pictures that illustrate the word "dream" according to my online searches or whatever data Google collects from my online activities.

Among the top search results, I found

- a portrait of John Lennon, with a quote from the best-selling single of his solo career "Imagine,"
- Pablo Picasso's painting "Le Rêve" ("The Dream"),
- a portrait of the smiling Marilyn Monroe,
- Henri Rousseau's painting "Le Rêve" ("The Dream"), and

- black and white photographs showing Martin Luther King delivering his "I have a Dream"-speech

This diverse array of pictures may very well illustrate the subconscious reason why so many of us have difficulties with the slogan "Will you be living the life of your dreams?"

Here are the facts:

- Most people can't visualize either one of the two world-famous paintings.
- Probably, in the sixties, most men did not dream of Marilyn Monroe but rather fantasized about her.
- John Lennon asked us to *"imagine"* a world without heaven or hell, no countries or possessions, and all people sharing the world; sadly, it seems that we are just as far away from this imagination as we were in 1971 when Lennon recorded his song. And, the way it looks this imagination will always stay an imagination.

*

In our minds, all of these *"dreams"* Google Images presented to me are somewhat **vague** with the exception of one: Martin Luther King's deliverance of his "I Have a Dream" speech.

It is real to everybody in this country and in the whole world. When we hear the words "I Have a Dream," all of us see the same picture in our minds. It shows Martin Luther King standing on the steps of the Lincoln Memorial, delivering his famous speech to over 250,000 civil rights supporters on August 28, 1963. There is nothing vague about it. Martin Luther King delivered his dream, and people followed his vision.

While many people might look at a picture or a postcard of Pablo Picasso's painting "Le Rêve" and never guess that its sales price of $155 million is rumored to be the highest price paid for an artwork by a U.S. collector, this black and white photograph speaks to all of us.

We know exactly what it depicts, what Dr. King dreamed about, that the people in this picture shared his dream, and that this dream became a reality. Even elementary school students in America can describe what this picture shows. This picture not only depicts a dream, but it also shows real success.

This picture also points to a specific facet of success. **Success does not come from having a dream; it comes from showing up in person and being invested.**

Though it is clear that Dr. King must have dreamed *the dream* his entire life, he did not just "have a dream" and speak about it; he became invested into the dream. After Rosa Park's arrest in 1955, Martin Luther King led the Montgomery Bus Boycott Movement. It lasted 381 days, longer than one year. During this period, thousands of African Americans walked thousands of miles by foot to boycott the city of Montgomery's city transit system. The organizers of the boycott arranged for private transportation to far away locations, raised funds, and even collected new and slightly used shoes to replace footwear worn out from walking long distances. Dr. King's, as well Civil Rights Movement leader Ralph Abernathy's houses, were firebombed, and Dr. King got arrested. How much more invested can one get?

Conquering this critical phase created the momentum to make *the dream* a reality, even before the speech was conceived and delivered, seven years later.

Another notable dream was the moon landing.

Again, a speech was delivered, this time by a president. Thousands of scientists worked around the clock, astronauts risked their lives, and hundreds of millions of people stopped everything they did to watch Neil Armstrong set foot on the moon and to listen to his words.

Again, another dream was the Berlin Wall coming down to unite German people again.

Hundreds of people died trying to escape over the wall; President Kennedy declared himself a Berliner, President Reagan called upon President Gorbachev to tear down this wall, and finally, thousands of people showed up with sledge hammers to actually tear down that wall.

Naturally, not all dreams-coming-true received the same attention.

Only five people witnessed the Wright Brothers' first flight at Kitty Hawk, North Carolina, on December 17, 1903.

But still, if we are honest about it, all of us know that for something to be "a dream," it has to BIG, really BIG, and it has to **benefit others**.

That's why listening to the slogans

- Will you be living the life of your dreams?
- Catapult yourself toward the life you've always dreamed of!
- Bring your dreams to life – now!

... and similar slogans can cause a problem.

There is no "will you be living...", there is no "catapulting," and there is no "now" when it comes to dreams.

Real dreams grow organically.

African Americans had been treated unjustly for hundreds of years, during which *the dream* became the dream.

Considering that hundreds of generations looked at the moon almost every night, it can't be a surprise that people wondered about constructing a vehicle that would allow them to fly and to reach this moon which seemed so close. In reality, man went from taking the first flight (1903) to the successful launching of the first artificial Earth satellite (Sputnik, 1957) in barely more than half a century, an unprecedented achievement that shows the scale of the dream.

The reverse situation was the reason for the tearing down of the Berlin Wall. Germans, who still remembered being united, wanted that wall to come down and be together again with their loved ones and friends from "the other side."

All of these dreams are collective dreams; many people dreamed of them together, which helped make them a reality.

Other dreams may not have been collective dreams, but they became collective dreams. A good list to search for the people who dreamed these dreams is the list of the Nobel Prize winners. Some of these dreams happened so long ago that today, people don't even know how they got started.

For instance, in 1859, Henri Dunant's idea of helping wounded soldiers without regard to their side in a military conflict and establishing neutrality protections for doctors and nurses must have seemed outright crazy, yet he founded the Red Cross and received the first-ever Nobel Peace Prize for this achievement. Over the centuries the Red Cross expanded on its goals. Today, with hundreds of environmental and other catastrophes per year, the Red Cross is more relevant than ever.

DREAMS are BIG or even HUGE; therefore, owning a big house or driving a red luxury car is not a dream but a goal.

This semantic difference makes *all the difference* with regards to our long and short term approaches to achieving success.

If we pursue a "real dream," we cannot get disillusioned. A real dream cannot become "not that important." If one of the pursuers dies, another one will rise in his/her place and keep on going. But, writing a bestseller, buying a 12,000 square feet house with stainless steel appliances, or becoming CFO at some company just isn't the same thing. That is why the concept of the dream bestseller, the dream job, and the dream house only works if their pursuers go about it like J.K. Rowling, Steve Jobs, and Mark Zuckerberg. And, these "dreamers" did not dream a dream when they set out to make their mark in history.

DREAMS VS. GOALS

dream

(1): an idea or vision that is created in your imagination and that is not real
(2): something that you have wanted very much to do, be, or have for a long time

***

goal

(1): the result or achievement toward which effort is directed; aim;

Synonyms
   1. target; purpose, object, objective, intent, intention.
   2. finish.

[Please notice that the word "dream" is NOT a synonym for the word "goal"!]

***

Let's examine the difference of semantics as it applies to this book with a symbolic example.

Edmund Hillary may have **dreamed** about being the first person to conquer Mount Everest, as did many others. But, what if he hadn't achieved it? Would it still have been *his* dream? Most certainly, it was Hillary's **goal** to conquer Mountain Everest, and accordingly he was invested, training for this feat.

Once Edmund Hillary and Tenzing Norgay reached the summit, the **dream** became true, not only for Hillary and Norgay but for the whole community of mountain climbers; now all of them knew that the highest mountain in the world could be conquered.

The **dream** even became a dream-come-true for mankind, because it showed what extraordinary actions humans are capable of, thereby encouraging all to strive for achieving new goals.

*

Let's look at a few other extremely successful people, whose goals achieved dream status:

When Steve Jobs and Steve Wozniak began building motherboards in Jobs' parents' garage, there was no dream of the famous "Think different" commercial (1997), which showed the "dreamers" Albert Einstein, Bob Dylan, Martin Luther King, Jr., Richard Branson, John Lennon & Yoko Ono, Buckminster Fuller, Thomas Edison, Muhammad Ali, Ted Turner, Maria Callas, Mahatma Gandhi, Amelia Earhart, Alfred Hitchcock, Martha Graham, Jim Henson, Frank Lloyd Wright, and Pablo Picasso.
[This is the complete list of "dreamers" according to Steve Jobs.]

In fact, there wasn't even a dream of the famous "1984" commercial. In 1976, the two Steves had just **one goal** – to build and sell the "best computer." They were invested in their goal, they talked others into being a part of it, and eventually, a dream of creating products that are intuitively easy to use took shape.

Equally, Mark Zuckerberg did not dream of building the world's largest social media platform with two billion active users per month when he created Facebook in his dorm room in 2004; he *merely* wanted to create a cool social media platform for Harvard University students. **That's a goal and not a dream.**

Eventually, Facebook was expanded to colleges in the Boston area and, since 2006, anyone who fulfills the age requirement can become a registered user of the website. Today, Facebook Inc. employs many thousands of people worldwide and injects billions of dollars into various countries' economies.

Somebody is dreaming now!

Even though neither Apple Inc. nor Facebook Inc. began as a dream their founders achieved dream success status because they conquered very specific goals, one after the other, successfully.

The same principle can also be applied to personal goals.

OTHER GOALS THAT TURNED INTO DREAMS

*"**Twenty years from now** you will be more disappointed by the things that you didn't do than by the ones you did do. So throw off the bowlines. Sail away from the safe harbor. Catch the trade winds in your sails. Explore. Dream. Discover."* – Mark Twain

I took this picture of the Potala Palace in Lhasa, Tibet, on January 14, 1987. It was long before I ever heard the quote.

By chance, I captured a symbolic view of what was to come – a dark cloud was hanging over the Potala, which is the symbol of Tibet and sacred symbolism of the religious struggle for purification.

Today, everybody considers my trip to Tibet a dream vacation. I got to see the magic of Tibet long before thousands of tourists invaded it and thereby changed how it felt to be in Tibet.

In reality, I never thought of it as a dream vacation until many years later. In fact, I regretted that I did not get an opportunity to see more of Tibet; I planned on returning and devoting at least two months to the exploration of Tibet. In my opinion, this 1987 trip made me only realize how much more time I wanted to spend there.

As a young teenager, I'd met Austrian mountaineer Heinrich Harrer, the teacher of the Dalai Lama and author of *"Seven Years in Tibet,"* in person, when he toured my home country with his book. After listening to his presentation, I had waited in line to get my copy of his book signed. I wasn't even twelve years old then. When Harrer signed my book, he asked me whether I considered visiting Tibet. Naturally, I said, "Yes." His stories of this *magical place* would have gotten almost anybody to say "Yes."

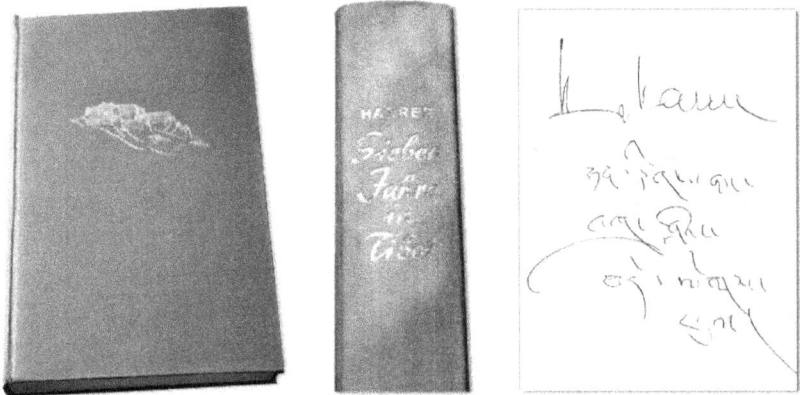

Telling the great man that "YES, I would travel" was almost like a contract, and most certainly, it became a goal. Harrer told me to hurry up because the Chinese would change Tibet. Twelve years later, I had the chance, and I went.

To reach Tibet I flew via plane from an altitude of 1,200 feet above sea elevation to 12,000 feet. The air is very thin up there.

There was no transportation; I had to walk everywhere by foot including to the top of the Potala Palace where the Dalai Lama's former suite is located. The Potala Palace is thirteen stories or 384 ft high. It took me thirty minutes to walk up there because the air is so thin that people who are not accustomed can hardly breathe. At my hotel stayed three tourists who had been in Lhasa for more than a week but had been unable to walk up the Potala's steep stairs.

Aside from dealing with altitude sickness, there was no infrastructure to support any problems tourists might have. Tourists who got really sick had to rest in their hotel rooms. There was no hospital for foreigners, and there were no English-speaking doctors, tourist guides, or even hotel personnel. In other words, everybody was on their own.

The dilapidated building in the foreground of my picture of the Potala is my hotel. It had no heating (I visited during January), no bathroom attached, and the snowy roof on the right side of the picture is the roof of the common outhouse and showers.

There weren't even any souvenirs.

But nothing could bother me. I had reached my goal – literally. [Tibet is often called the "Roof of the World."]

I was invested in the idea (by wish and by "contract with Harrer") that I would get to Tibet and see it, one way or the other, and so I succeeded.

Traveling to Tibet at a time when only a handful of people per day made it there, I got a chance to meditate in the Dalai Lama's bedroom alone by myself, for thirty minutes. There wasn't anybody there who would have hindered me in doing that. It was an unexpected, spiritual gift for which I'll always be grateful.

Even though I thought I could repeat this trip any day, it did not happen. Instead, it turned out that Harrer had been right. The Chinese opened Tibet to mass tourism. In 2005, the Chinese managed to complete the Qinghai–Tibet railway, which features the world's highest railway station (16,627 ft above sea level) and the world's highest rail tunnel (16,093 ft above sea level). Of course, in 1987, and even much later it was unthinkable that such a railroad could be built.

Starting in 2006 tourists began traveling to Tibet in huge numbers. While I was observing from a distance, the Tibet I had experienced vanished. Since then, every day up to 2,300 visitors are being ushered through the Dalai Lama's bedroom, where I had stood in reverence, listening to the sounds, and watching the winds pull the sheer orange curtains out of the window as if they wanted to connect the room with heaven.

Remember Mark Twain's quote? He spoke of "Twenty years from now... " In reality, construction of the new railroad was completed only eighteen years after I arrived in Tibet. My dream vacation can never be repeated.

(modern Lhasa)

Especially, when I tell spiritual people that I got a chance to meditate in the Dalai Lama's bedroom, they almost faint while exclaiming "Oh my God, I can't believe that... You made a dream come true... "

Nothing could be further from the truth. At the time I was twenty-four years old, a tough cookie who worked in the movie industry sixteen hours per day. I also believed and was invested in the idea that if we really want something we'll make it happen, which is what I did. Because I did not even expect to have an otherworldly experience, I scheduled only a five-day stay in Tibet and had to leave even though I didn't want to.

It was being there and experiencing the serenity, spirituality, and peace of Tibet that opened up my interest in the teachings of Buddhism, and not the other way around.

I did not have a dream when I began the journey; I had a goal. It ended up becoming a dream come true.

The same can be said for much, much bigger dreams.

I speculate that when Henry Dunant, the founder of the Red Cross, arrived in Solferino, Italy on the evening of June 24, 1859, he did not have a dream of founding an international humanitarian organization with millions of volunteers who help to prevent and lessen human suffering. Dunant was a social activist who traveled to Solferino because it was the location of a decisive battle in the Second Italian War of Independence.

Once there, Dunant saw 23,000 wounded, dying and dead soldiers lying on a battlefield, with nobody helping the survivors. Dunant organized the civilian population, especially the women and girls, to assist the injured soldiers. He also organized the purchase of needed materials and helped in building makeshift hospitals. That's how the Red Cross got started. Only, that was before it was called the Red Cross.

We have also established that neither Steve Jobs nor Mark Zuckerberg started their companies with a dream.

Though motivational books, videos, and speeches often name Bill Gates, Henry Ford, Oprah Winfrey, Walt Disney, Michael Jordan, Steve Jobs, Stephen King, and J.K. Rowling among the group of people who had a dream and who succeeded after failure, we have to wonder, "Did these ridiculously successful people really have a dream or did they have a series of goals that led to a dream come true?"

I believe if we assume that all these people **got invested in their respective fields, and then built upon individual successes, it is much easier to see why they became so successful.**

Whereas the dreams of setting foot on the moon or giving African Americans equal rights were hundreds of years old, it is safe to assume that J.K. Rowling just wanted to publish a novel about a fictitious young magician named Harry Potter and that Bill Gates became fascinated with computers as a teenager and kept on building success upon success.

To succeed we do not have to have a dream; it is more than enough if we have one goal like shooting perfect hoops (Michael Jordan) or building a car everyone could afford (Henry Ford).

Still, when we follow the *right* goals, personal or professional, they often turn into dreams come true as a matter of course.

CAN ONE DREAM THEIR WAY OUT OF JAIL (METAPHORICALLY SPEAKING)?

So far we have learned about a scientist who was so invested in his research that he felt he had to save his scientific samples under life-threatening danger, a media mogul who cared more about winning a race than considering that it might cost him his life, two authors who wanted to push their books to reach bestseller status, a civil rights activist who had the real dream of securing legal rights for African Americans, a social rights activist who wanted to save injured soldiers, and me, who just wanted to see Heinrich Harrer's magical Tibet. With the exception of one of the authors, all of us reached their goals.

But what about people who are with their back to the wall, ten times over, people who are in prison for a good reason?

*

Coss Marte grew up in the Lower Eastside where, in the eighties, drugs were sold at every corner. At age thirteen, he became a drug dealer. At twenty-three, he was a kingpin making two millions dollars per year and – going to prison, for the second time.

There, the heavily overweight, chain-smoking father of a two year old learned from the prison doctor that his health was so bad that he'd probably die within five years while still in prison. At which point Coss Marte decided that he was not going to die "in this place" because his son needed him. Coss began working out the same day.

He created his own workout program which could be done without equipment in a six by nine-foot prison cell. Not only did he lose seventy pounds in six months but also helped twenty other inmates lose over one thousand pounds. Shortly before he was supposed to be released, he had an experience that made him realize that, on a larger scale, his drug-dealing caused damage to his community. He then devised a plan to give back and help. Since he was able to coach fifty other inmates to lose weight, he decided he was going to become a personal trainer.

Unfortunately, once released, Coss had to find out that no gym wanted to hire him. As soon as he filled out a job application, in which he had to admit that he had been in prison, the job interview was over.

But, Coss didn't give up. He was invested in staying clean, being healthy, and doing something good for his community. If he could not get hired, he would just have to start his own business. Coss printed business cards, handed them out on the street to people who were wearing jogging pants, and started working out in parks. Eventually, he was able to rent studios. As his business grew, he hired his first employee – another ex-convict.

Today, Coss Marte employs sixteen people, twelve of whom are ex-convicts. He is breaking down stereotypes, helping former prisoners to get a new start in life. And he speaks about it to help our society understand what's at stake. Even better, he is really good at what he's doing. One of Coss's ConBody studios is located at Saks Fifth Avenue, and he also presented a TEDTalk.

Just like Mark Zuckerberg's goal of creating a cool social media platform for Harvard students evolved, Coss Marte's goal of working as a personal trainer evolved. He is well on his way to achieving his dream. Beyond being invested in what he's doing, he also chose a socially responsible goal. People love to support entrepreneurs who pursue goals that make an impact on others and society itself.

MAKING *EVERYTHING YOU KNOW* WORK FOR YOU

When we look at Coss Marte's story or the immense successes of Mark Zuckerberg, E.L. James and other overnight sensations it becomes clear that any form of "traditional path" to success died with the end of the last century.

Still, something is to be learned from a man who achieved his unbelievable success by following the traditional path. You have probably never heard of him unless you work in the hotel industry.

This man was born in 1850, the youngest of thirteen children, in a poor peasant family in Switzerland. Not a particularly outstanding student, he apprenticed as a sommelier, then moved to Paris, where he worked as a waiter, then restaurant manager, and then floor waiter of the Hôtel Splendide in Paris, one of the most lavish hotels in Europe at the time.

After a short stint in my hometown Vienna at the time of the International Exhibition, he became the director of a restaurant in Nice, France. Onwards he moved as the maître d'hôtel of the Grand Hotel in Locarno, and eventually, manager of the Grand Hotel National in Lucerne, Switzerland. At the same time, he also held the same position at the Grand Hôtel in Monaco. Only eleven years after he began working in the industry, this man managed two hotels from the same chain in two different countries (in 1878, even before telephones came into use). Finally, in 1896, the former poor peasant son formed a hotel syndicate. His name?

César Ritz.

Among the hotels from his syndicate are the Hôtel Ritz in Paris, where Princess Diana used to stay when she visited the city, and The Ritz Hotel in London. Ritz's nickname was "king of hoteliers, and hotelier to kings." The term ritzy is derived from his name and that of his hotels.

*

It is doubtful that César Ritz chose his career. A peasant's child who did not excel in school, he was probably placed in his environment by chance. He had to learn on the job. There were no colleges teaching gastronomic sciences then. That meant that César Ritz had to search for answers, stay focused, and be invested.

Here are some of the success formulas César Ritz applied:

- **Decide what you want!**

[By chance placed in the hospitality industry, César Ritz wanted to succeed in this industry. Early in his career, he got fired from the Hotel de la Fidélité for breaking too many dishes in his desire to work quick; no doubt, he learned from that experience.]

- **Have a Vision!**

[César Ritz had a vision of the best customer experience like nobody else. He created a new "gold standard" of quality and unparalleled service excellence that still stands today.]

- **Work harder than you ever thought you could!**

[César Ritz took great efforts to learn from the best. For instance, he made sure he'd be in Vienna for the International Exhibition 1873, an astonishing insight for a 23-year old who came from humble beginnings. He recognized it as a chance to meet with people from the entire world who traveled to Vienna to see new state-of-the-art science and technology. Since all foreigners had to stay at hotels and eat at restaurants working in Vienna gave César the opportunity to study the needs of people from different cultures he would not have met otherwise.]

- **Dream Big!**

[César Ritz dreamed of creating a legendary customer experience, and today we know that he created standards which are still relevant today, 125 years later.]

An obvious question is, how did a poor peasant boy manage to become the "king of hoteliers, and hotelier to kings"?

I believe César Ritz wasn't just ambitious, hard-working, and enterprising like many other young men. In addition to these qualities, César Ritz turned his personal situation into his greatest strength. He knew the value of "feeling special" before he learned anything about hotels, and he built on this knowledge.

Born in 1850, long before consumerism became a thing, César Ritz was most likely the recipient of hundreds of hand-me-downs; after all, he was the youngest of thirteen children. We can imagine that, at times, others made fun of his clothing or lack of neat school supplies. One must also assume that, often, César's siblings ordered him around because that's what older siblings do. Consequently, César Ritz learned the value of small, considerate acts that make people feel special. Focusing on paying attention to even the smallest details allowed him to create a legendary customer experience.

As a manager, he was the first to instruct "the customers is always right" and "If a diner complains about a dish or the wine, immediately remove it and replace it, no questions asked."

The lesson to be learned is that all of us have special know-how we can make work for us. Most likely, in the future, huge success will be tied to being able to create emotions and feel good experiences because that is something Artificial Intelligence (AI) will always lack.

BAD INVESTMENTS, INCLUDING FROM COMPANIES

What's to do if people don't even have a goal because they feel stuck in a dead-end job and stuck in life? Maybe they also do not have the money to go to college, though there is no excuse for not getting an education. The Internet is free and full of educational offerings from Wikipedia to TED videos. All it takes is getting invested according to our personal likings and learning styles.

People who are stuck need to keep their eyes open to spot opportunities. Chances are they are surrounded by people who feel equally stuck, which increases the chance that the one who stays on the lookout for opportunities will score. I knew a woman who kept her eyes open but then failed miserably.

Thirty years ago, this lady, let's call her Bertha, worked a low-end job at a pharmaceutical company that was involved in early HIV/AIDS research. Bertha was her parents' only child, but when she wanted to go college and study engineering, her father denied her wish. He wanted her to make a career in sales because in his opinion "women weren't meant to study engineering." Bertha obliged. Her attempts to still make it into any field closer to what she wanted to do failed; she only managed to get hired at that dead-end job at the pharmaceutical company. But she kept her eyes open.

And so she noticed that when HIV/AIDS patients came in, the research assistants would measure the boils the patients had with a plastic ruler just like the ones elementary school students use in class. Each boil was carefully measured with a separate new ruler to avoid any cross contamination. At the time, people did not know too much about HIV/AIDS. After measuring each boil, the research assistants threw the plastic ruler into a garbage can for hazardous waste and took a new ruler to measure the next boil.

It wasn't Bertha's job to think about this procedure because Bertha had the dead-end job. Still, Bertha kept her eyes open and thought about the things she saw. Mind you, this was a pharmaceutical company. There were people making really nice wages. If Bertha could have gone to college, she might have been able to get the job of a research assistant at least. Bertha harbored negative feelings; she was invested in the pain her father caused when he would not allow her to study engineering. She also did not like the people, who had the good jobs. In a way, she wanted to show them that she was more talented. And, Bertha really was.

Then, one day it happened. Bertha opened her mouth and said what she had been thinking, "Why don't you print a ruler on paper and save the expense for the plastic rulers?"

How amazingly simple and brilliant!

*

The pharmaceutical company saved hundreds of thousands of dollars. And, Bertha? Bertha got a plaque and a gift certificate.

When Bertha told me the story, I blurt out, "Oh my God! Why did you not go to a lawyer and ask how you should present this so you would get appropriate compensation?"

"Well," said Bertha, "I knew that when I got hired I had to sign a trailer clause, which gave my employer rights to inventions made by any employee, including up to six months *after* employees left the job. It is a standard clause at that company."

"AAAND?" I said, "Why didn't you wait tables or clean houses? Or, whatever? You had a windfall in the amount of six figures coming. Surely that would have been worth biting into the sour apple for six months. You could have claimed that you 'dreamed about' this invention seven months after you quit working there."

Bertha never talked to me again. She hated me. I made the mistake of saying out loud what she thought ever since she received the (stupid) plaque. I saw her from time to time; she became a really bitter woman. The simple truth is Bertha got invested in her anger. She spent decades proving that if her father would have let her, she *could have* been somebody instead of using her intelligence to move where she wanted to be.

But, what's worse than this remarkable story is that it happens again and again, every day. Some companies' practices of not paying their employees enough money create conditions, in which employees become disillusioned and stop being invested in their careers. Employees who get and stay invested can improve their career simply because those around them don't.

Michael worked at one of the print shops where I used to get my work printed. The company had invested into a complete renovation of the store. Also, the store was going to get a new manager. On the surface, it was looking as if the company was upping the game. Michael had applied to become manager, but he himself did not think that he stood a chance. In the past, he had been denied a promotion twice. Michael was invested in the anger about this situation.

After the renovation, the print shop where he worked also began to offer ink cartridges, pens, and related merchandise. Therefore, customers needed to line up between the four new sales racks which had been set up parallel to the counter. That made it a bit difficult for customers to form proper lines because there wasn't really that much space.

On a busy Friday, I happened to be there, the last person in line. By the time I made it to the counter, only Michael and I were left at the store. The other employee had clocked out and left according to his schedule.

"Saw this BS?" Michael said to me and gestured towards the sales floor. I had known Michael for a long time. We were friends.

"What BS?" I asked.

"These idiots!" Michael said and gestured back toward the company's logo on the wall. "They are so stupid! They should turn the sales racks 90 degrees. That way the customers could form nice lines between the shelves, and if they have to wait like today, maybe they'd pick up one or other pen or spend some money on that useless merchandise."

I turned around and looked at the new sales racks. No doubt, Michael was right. Turning the sales racks would improve the spatial distribution and display the merchandise so customers could actually see it while they had to wait in line.

"BAM," I said, "Nobody noticed that yet?"

"Nope!" said Michael, "And I won't tell them. Why would I? They have overlooked me long enough!"

At no point did it occur to Michael that this simple observation might help him to prove that he could be the best manager. He was invested in his anger that he had been overlooked. He applied the success formulas by proving to himself that, indeed, his employer was totally incompetent because time and again, they hurt themselves by not promoting competent people who cared about the business.

The company hired somebody from out of town to become manager. That gentleman was truly incompetent – by my standards. Once, I happened to be at the store and asked him to run an oversized scan from one of my own books. The manager did not ask me if I had permission to scan this picture even though he could not know that I owned the copyright. I could also prove it, but he did not ask me to prove it. Scanning a picture without asking for copyright permission and putting it on a customer's flash drive is a crystal-clear copyright violation forbidden by business standards. Michael would have known that, but he was so angry that by the time this happened, he had found another job at another printing company where he worked the same dead-end job as before, only at a different shop and under a different manager.

*

It is easy to think that Bertha and Michael were not invested in their own cause, but what about the companies? Both, Bertha and Michael, left their respective jobs to work other dead-end jobs but the companies, who did not invest in these two smart people, lost them altogether.

Obviously, both, Bertha and Michael, could have been much more "successful in the eyes of society" if they would have been more invested in their careers instead of their anger.

Then again, both of them worked for companies where they had direct managers, district managers, human resources managers, and somewhat way up there CEOs and boards, who set policies and made sure that they were enforced. All of them failed miserably for their companies even though they had more resources.

Clearly, Bertha's employer acted shortsighted when they gave her a plaque (How about a Cartier watch?) and a gift certificate. If Bertha could see things that were overlooked by higher-paid employees in higher ranks, shouldn't Bertha have been promoted to become somewhat of an observer who just spent time in various departments as an outsider, to look for ways the company could save money? She did not need a degree for that; she had already proven herself. In the short time she spent there, she saved them hundreds of thousands of dollars. How much more could she have done for the company if they had gotten "invested" in furthering their extremely talented employees?

Until 2013, one of the most successful companies in the world, Google, asked their employees to spend time every week to work on their own ideas, which allowed them to develop innovations like Gmail and AdSense. Equally, Apple has Blue Sky, which allows some workers to work on special projects they come up with on their own, and Microsoft has The Garage program.

By investing in their employees, companies become more successful companies because they too need to be invested, not only their employees.

THE RELIGIOUS-PHILOSOPHICAL ASPECT

Let's look again at my sentence,

"... The simple truth is Bertha got invested in her anger. She spent decades proving that if her father would have let her, she *could have* been somebody instead of using her intelligence to move where she wanted to be..."

Whether you are religious or an atheist, you probably know that *all* great religions ask us "to forgive others." While at a first glance this concept looks like some altruistic idea that invites us "to give up a feeling we are entitled to" it really isn't.

Everybody knows somebody who is so invested in his/her anger that he or she just cannot see the opportunities beyond. Had Bertha taken the position, "OK, my dad is an old-fashioned, 19th century type of guy; it's really too bad... Now, that we know that... What do I have to do to get into college?", undoubtedly she would have succeeded.

Instead, Bertha got invested in her anger. Every time she outscored somebody with pure intelligence and understanding of technical concepts, Bertha put another notch on the barrel, successfully. ["... *See, Dad, I would have had what it takes...*"]

Bertha should have forgiven her father to be able to move on and be successful the way she wanted to be successful.

That is why absolutely all great religions urge people to forgive others. Getting invested in anger, or also in the seven deadly sins (wrath, greed, sloth, pride, lust, envy, and gluttony), keeps us from being invested in what matters for our success. There are only so and so many opportunities in our paths and so and so many hours in the day.

THE GAMBLING ASPECT

Lots of us gamble; we buy lottery tickets and scratch-off tickets. The concept is, "if you don't buy a ticket, you can't win." In other words, if you don't risk a few dollars you don't even have a chance to become "successful" and win "the big pot."

I don't buy lottery tickets, but I do gamble on success.

Yes, it is true that if you don't buy a ticket, you can't win the big pot; equally, it is true that if you don't apply for the job, you can't get the job. And, if you don't ask the girl out, she won't go on a date with you, because she does not know that you are interested, just like the Human Resources manager does not know that you want the job.

Now, let's compare the odds of getting the job to winning the lottery. Obviously, your odds of succeeding in getting the job are always better, because never ever will 258+ million people apply for any job.

1: 258,890,850 are the odds to win a huge jackpot.

258,890,850 is a number higher than the number of people who are legally allowed to work in the United States.

But, what's even better is that, contrary to playing the lottery, everybody can get invested in "getting the job" and **improve their odds**.

Though sometimes it appears that "the little people" face the worst odds of getting hired, that's not really so. Quite the opposite is true, but stars are better at hiding their emotions when they don't win.

Thirty-one actresses and movie stars auditioned for the role of Scarlett O'Hara in *Gone with the Wind* (1939). Clearly, the odds of

31:1 don't look so bad at all, in comparison to playing the lottery. Also, "the prize" was better than winning the lottery.

Famous movie star Paulette Goddard did nine screen tests. At the time she was married to Charlie Chaplin (Talk about connections.) Quite obviously, Paulette Goddard got invested. She "owned 9 tickets (nine screen tests)." But it was British actress Vivien Leigh who took home the prize, got to play Scarlett, and won her first Oscar for Best Actress. Was Paulette Goddard angry that she did not win the prize? I don't know, but if she was, Goddard did not invest in that anger. She shot four movies in the relevant years 1938-1939.

For an actor or an actress, getting invested and "gambling on success" does not stop at getting the role. Supposedly, actress Halle Berry did not shower for an entire month so that she could play the role of a crack addict in the movie "Jungle Fever" convincingly. It became one of her break-through roles.

And, even though Robert De Niro had already won an Academy Award for Best Supporting Actor, he registered for a taxi driver's license and worked 12 hours a day for weeks in preparation for his role in the critically acclaimed movie "Taxi Driver."

It is important to understand that all these efforts of "getting invested" are gambles, too. How many movies have flopped at the box office? Moviegoers could have rejected "Taxi Driver" because it is a violent movie, or hundreds of other things could have happened that could have hindered its success.

Would Halle Berry have felt bad about not showering for a month if that role were not a breakthrough role?

Would Robert de Niro have regretted working as a taxi driver had the audience rejected the movie?

I don't think so because these actors decided to take a gamble, get fully invested, and apply the success formulas

- Decide what you want!
- Have a Vision!
- Do It!
- Work harder than you ever thought you could!
- Don't be Afraid to Fail!

Most people who gamble envision what they would do **IF** they'd win. I used to work with a gambler. Every Friday he told me what he'd do if he'd win on Saturday; most importantly, that he'd not come back to work on Monday.

However, contrary to the above mentioned actors and actresses, he could not get invested in his gamble. All he could do was to buy the ticket and wait, whereas Halle Berry could and did visit a crack den with a police officer as her escort and then decided not to shower for a month.

Naturally, getting invested means taking a risk. How many of us managed to get hired for what we thought would be a dream job only to find out that though the manager with whom we interviewed was a likable fellow, a new colleague with whom we had to work daily was a most annoying person?

Again, the same might also be true for movie stars, though usually covered in a shroud of glamour and glitz. It's probably a bit scary to visit a crack den. Similarly, Robert de Niro might have driven people who threw up in his cab.

The bottom line is that we can't buy tickets for reaching the dream but have to take the gamble of getting invested in what we believe in and then

- Do It!

- Work harder than you ever thought you could! (and)
- Don't be Afraid to Fail!

THE SLIGHTLY DANGEROUS SUCCESS FORMULA

One of the many success formulas needs to be applied with caution. It's the slogan about "getting up again" – words to the effect that never mind how often life knocks us down, we have to get up again...

This slogan is only partially true.

Of course, the analogy stems from boxing, which proves that the saying is only partially true. The goal in boxing is not to "get up again as often as possible." As defined by the rules of boxing it is every fighter's goal to score as many punches, jabs, crosses, hooks, and uppercuts as possible. Fighters are awarded points for winning rounds by "connecting more often." The fighter who earns more points will win the fight. Because it is hard to knock down or even knock out an opponent, more fighters stay victorious by winning on points than by scoring a knock out.

In contrast to other success formulas, *"Get up, when life knocks you down!"* is very easy to visualize. Among other boxing movies, the *"Rocky"* series presented unforgettable visuals, even to people who don't watch professional boxing. These memorable visuals show a bloodied fighter lying on the ground, with a referee kneeling next to him and hitting the floor with his fist while performing the mandatory count.

But that's not how boxing happens. In the real world of boxing, no referee would allow a seriously hurt and bloodied fighter to continue. Also, typically, fighters don't just stand there and wait to get hit; they try to adjust their strategy before they get knocked down or out.

Whether you are a boxing fan, or not, you have probably seen one of the most talked-about fights of the last century: "invincible" Mike Tyson getting knocked out by Buster Douglas. Even if you are too young to have watched this memorable fight on February 10, 1990, you might have seen a re-run or one of the "anniversary airings."

Most interestingly, though all viewers remember the visual of Mike Tyson looking for his mouth piece, on his knees, quite disorientated, in the 10th round, rarely anybody remembers the visual of Buster Douglas **"getting knocked down and getting up"** in the 8th.

That's how the success formula of "getting up again" should be understood and applied.

Buster Douglas got invested in the fight. Mind you, Douglas could have put on a show for a round or two, then gone down, taken the best payday of his life, and carried on. Probably, quite a few people in the Tyson camp thought that that's what Douglas would do. But, it wasn't not what Douglas elected to do. Douglas got invested and trained for this fight like nobody else did. He applied the success formulas

- Decide what you want!
- Have a Vision!
- Work harder than you ever thought you could!
- Believe in yourself!
- Try the Impossible!

Since Douglas did all of this, he was the man who could pull off the success formula "Get up when life knocks you down!" — successfully!!!

And, the funny thing is: Nobody even remembers it.

Just ask anybody over the age of fifty about the Tyson vs. Douglas fight. People will give you lengthy descriptions of how decisively Douglas knocked down Tyson; some people will tell you that as soon as they saw Douglas enter the ring, they knew... *[Really?...]*

You can even ask people what they thought when Douglas went down, and people will immediately tell you that you are mistaken because it was Tyson who went down (not Buster Douglas) and that Tyson lost the fight. But, in fact, Douglas did go down in the 8th even though nobody remembers his "getting knocked down and getting up."

"Getting up again" only works if we are fully invested, if our "getting up" is the logical consequence of our state of being invested. Fighters who get up too often, when they are not supposed to get up, suffer brain damage; some of them have even died.

Equally, any professional who gets "knocked-down" in their line of work too often may not be fully invested, maybe for the simple reason that their talents lie elsewhere. Instead of getting up again in the same line of work, it might be wiser to find out what they really want to be invested in and "Have a Vision!", "Believe in Yourself!", "Don't be Afraid to Fail!" and try what they were born to do.

We don't have to suffer, don't have to get knocked down over and over so we can get up again and again. In times like these, we have every opportunity to do what we want to be invested in. When we do what we were born to do, "getting up again" will come naturally to us just like it did for Buster Douglas.

BECAUSE IT'S THERE

People who suggest that anybody can make their dreams come true often use pictures of mountains to visualize what it takes to do so. Obviously, it feels like climbing a mountain.

Here are the three most famous words in mountaineering – "Because it's there!"

George Herbert Leigh Mallory, an English mountaineer who took part in the first three British expeditions to conquer Mount Everest in the early 1920s, uttered these words when he was asked, "Why do you want to climb Mount Everest? "

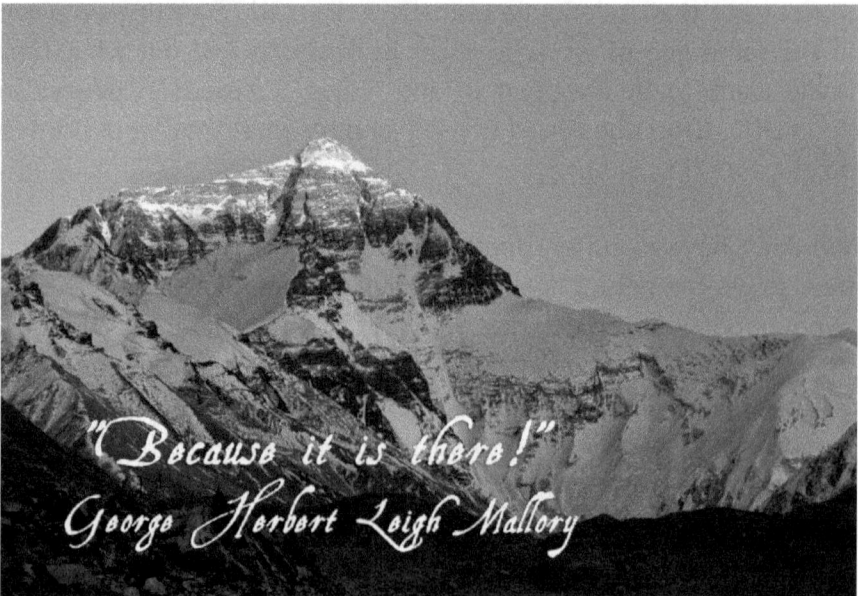

"Because it is there!"
George Herbert Leigh Mallory

"Because it's there!" may be the three most important words when it comes to moving on from achieving a goal to making a dream come true.

African Americans were discriminated for hundreds of years – the problem was "there." The moon was "up there" and so close; the

Berlin Wall was "there," in the way of people who wanted to be together. "There" were also the poor of the poorest in India who needed help from a woman who may be recognized as a saint during our lifetime. "There" were also diseases that killed people by the millions, with many more millions waiting for scientists to conquer these "highest mountains and deepest oceans" of problems...

"Because it's there!" is the battle cry for all of us to set goals and *maybe* get to dream the dream.

My dream trip to Tibet and my dream house, the little bungalow with white instead of stainless steel appliances, aren't even on the same chart.

Still, Tibet was "there" and waiting for me so I could tell the story and encourage others to go on the journey of their lifetime. And, my house was "there," on the market for over a year; nobody wanted to buy it because nobody wanted to invest so much work to save this jewel. If I hadn't done it, maybe it would have become rubble, added to a landfill.

But, "there" were also the plastic rulers. Opposite to thirty years ago, today, throwing away hundreds of thousands of plastic rulers would be considered an environmental catastrophe.

And, "there" were also the incorrectly set up shelves which affected the customers' comfort at the print shop.

"Because it's there" is the battle cry to get invested, become a player, and solve problems.

The world is moving forward, whether we participate or not.

SO, HOW DO WE SUCCEED?

Firstly, opposite to what the media and all kinds of organizations want to make us believe, success is deeply personal. Success isn't only "owned" by megastars, who live in estates and have a few million followers on Twitter. There is also the rest of us – the first child in a family to graduate from college, a plumber who left a huge company to set up his own small shop, the veteran who learned walking again with prosthetic limbs, the student who graduated and did not drop out, the couple, who raised their children well, lived healthy and enjoyed meeting not only their grandchildren but also their great-grandchildren.

*

Still, all of us know people who have "given up" or failed at something and never tried again. Because today's way of marketing pushes the idea that achieving any dream is possible, failing to "reach the dream" causes the kind of despair Zack experienced. This effect is exacerbated by the fact that all of us get inundated with sponsored social media postings which suggest that hundreds of people are making their dream come true the very moment when we see the ad.

In contrast, failing to reach a goal doesn't feel traumatic. We know that we only need to look for new and different solutions, just like Thomas Alva Edison.

Aiming to reach goal after goal frees us from the heaviness that comes with having to accomplish something epic. Instead it's like going to school. Nobody expects a student to accomplish something extraordinary, like getting into Harvard at age twelve. Everybody is happy if students just move along and take exam after exam until they graduate. And, if they fail along the way, it's good enough if they just retake the exam.

Forgetting about the dream and instead aiming to accomplish goal after goal is a time tested strategy for all.

AM I INVESTED IN MY LIFE THE WAY I NEED TO BE?

Over the past few years, I have asked hundreds of people what they thought about **why people failed to achieve their goals**. The most often articulated answer was, "Because people get side-tracked." And, it is true, I experienced it too.

When I renovated my house in Wilmington, North Carolina, every Sunday morning I got up and watched home improvement shows on HGTV at 8:00 a.m. I wasn't slacking; I was watching valuable information I needed. After "my shows" were finished, shows about "How to Renovate your Attic" and "How to Add Curb Appeal to Your Yard" came on. Comfortably, lying on the sofa, I watched these shows too, and even some more until my teenage children got up around 11:00 a.m.

But, I did not have an attic at my house, and I did not need to change my house's curb appeal. After a few weeks, it was time to ask the question, "Am I invested in *my* house renovation or in watching what *other people* do to their houses?"

To overcome the hurdle of getting sidetracked, we only need to ask ourselves:

Am I invested in my life the way I need to be?
with regards to family, friends, present employment, future employment, education or finding out what education might matter tomorrow, and so on... Obviously, there are thousands of scenarios.

Let's explore only one of the most common examples. In Gallup's

2013 State of the American Workplace study, 70 percent of participants checked off the field "disengaged" when it comes to their work.

That is not a good situation because "disengaged" employees aren't happy and they also don't "encourage" their employers to up their game. To become happier, "disengaged" employees could ask themselves: **HOW** am I invested in the company?

1. Does the company offer extraordinary benefits like a really good continuing education program that will help me to get a better job in the future?
2. Does the company offer excellent health insurance which I, my spouse, or one of my children depends on...
3. Is the company the only one of its kind in the city where my aging parents live, and though I could find a job in the next big city, visiting my parents from afar would add considerable hardship?
4. Will staying in this employment for one, two, or three years boost my resume?
5. Is there a chance that the department head I can't stand will leave or retire in the near future, which would make my employment a better career choice?

Next the employee should ask themselves: **HOW** am I invested in my specific job?

1. Am I invested in this **specific job** (but I am employed at the wrong company),
2. Am I invested in my **industry** (but I am not working the position I want to reach), or
3. Am I invested in my **earnings** (I don't really care what I do, I just want to make money)

Here is an example from my own employment history.

1. In 2006 I worked an underpaid job at a company where I had been promised a promotion from my direct manager. I got invested in the idea of this upcoming promotion (and in the company).

2. On the side, at home, I earned 124 credits at the company's internal continuing education academy in one calendar year. That was more than 10 course credits per month. Nobody asked me to do that.

3. I also earned the reputable Certiport Microsoft Office certification and paid for materials and test fees out of my pocket.

4. When finally the moment of promotion came, the person in charge messed up, and even though my direct manager supported me beyond my expectations, I did not get the job I wanted.

5. I was angry, really angry.

6. I had "held out" in this position under my skill level only because I had been promised a promotion. Not only had I patiently waited, I had made good use of the time and used the company's internal education system to add even more skills to my resume. But, with the exception of my direct manager, all other managers had decided to ignore my "being invested." That meant, they were not invested in my working for them.

7. I could not see how this situation could or would improve. Since obviously my direct manager's recommendations were ignored it did not look as if better things were waiting. Not only did the company not support me, they *also* did not value or support *her* judgment or recommendation.

8. Instead of indulging in my anger, I re-channeled that anger and wrote the best resume I have ever written, complete with a

portfolio on a CD, and applied for the *only* suitable job available in my town, at a construction company.

9. Not only did I apply for the job, I showed up in person to deliver the resume. This became key to getting the new job. The unnamed employer wanted resumes to be faxed to a fax number in Alabama where they had a project office. Have you ever tried tracking a project office's fax number? It is not easy, but after thirty minutes of research, I knew who the employer was and where their main office in my hometown was located. I donned my nicest coat and dropped off my resume.

10. The next day the vice president of the company called me personally to offer me a "better" job, one that was not even advertised. Owning the reputable Certiport Microsoft Office certification had done the trick. At the time only 2.5+ million people had it, worldwide. Also, by finding out name and address of the company and dropping off my resume, I had proven that I could find information, an extremely valuable skill in the construction industry. The interview was a formality.

11. Sadly, nine months later, when the marketing director left to pursue other interests, I was overlooked for getting this position. It wasn't that my bosses did not like me. It wasn't that I didn't have the credentials. Not only did I have the already described education, I also had a master's degree in a relevant field.

12. In reality, I did not get the job because of gender discrimination – in the year 2007. "Gisela, face it, construction is a man's world." Yep, that's what the owner of the company told me, but I had no witnesses.

13. The man who got hired instead of me was completely incompetent. He did not pull a single project ashore in six months. Eventually, somebody found out by accident that he played golf every Friday on company time.

14. Already two months into his tenure, I had a gut feeling that this guy could be instrumental in leading the company into bankruptcy. I tried to give him some pointers like to not pursue office upfits for financial companies because they were laying off people. He told me that I was wrong even though I showed him articles from the New York Times and the Washington Post. He had not figured out that we were sliding into a recession even though I could see it clearly.

15. I knew that if people were laid off, I would be in the first or second group. Since I was office personnel, I would be considered expendable.

16. Instead of investing in my anger that I had been gender discriminated (and the guy who got the job helped in running the company into the ground), I asked myself what I was invested in:

   a) I liked the company because they were extremely supportive of single moms. In fact, as a single mom, I had never received the kind of support all single moms received at this construction company.

   b) I really liked my job.

   c) I even liked almost all people who worked there, including Mr. Incompetent. He was funny; he just did not have any job qualities that would help in this difficult economic situation.

   d) For these reasons, I did not begin looking for another job as I had done before.

   e) I only hated that I had been discriminated and a totally incompetent guy had been hired instead of me being promoted. If the new hire would have been a whiz, I would have been happy to learn from him, gender discrimination or not.

f) Most importantly, I was invested in my family. As a widowed mother of two, I had to succeed.

17. To further my investment proactively, I devised a new marketing plan in secret, printed it and put it in a nice folder. I only did it secretly so Mr. Incompetent would not try to dismiss it before management could see the whole plan. Naturally, I invested hours of recreational time, but I knew I invested it in what really mattered.

18. At the next staff meeting, I waited for a chance to present my concept and left everybody in awe.

19. Still, it was too late. It was the beginning of the Great Recession. The banks were already shutting down. The CFO of the company could not get what we needed to pursue my plan. Three months later, I was laid off with a one-month severance pay. The company regretted to having to let me go; a few months later, they had to file for bankruptcy.

20. I found a new job within 36 days. With me, I brought my many skills nobody had told me to acquire but my being invested had pointed me there.

The same stupid things happen to all of us. Though I had my manager's support for the promotion at the first workplace, it did not happen. Though it is illegal, I got discriminated at the other job. Though I tried to help Mr. Incompetent, he did not want free help. Though I excelled in what I did, the economy and the Great Recession killed all my efforts to stay with the construction company.

The only reason why I kept afloat during this difficult period was because I was investing in my biggest cause, my professional life, so I could provide for my family.

Asking yourself **HOW** you are invested, in **WHAT** you are invested, and **WHAT** the next step is to further your investment is a much easier way to reach success than pondering

- Have a Vision!
- Believe in yourself!
- Don't be Afraid to Fail!

and of course

- Dream Big!

All these great slogans are equally vague as are the images Google showed in my search for pictures which illustrate "The Dream."

Asking yourself in **WHAT** you are invested, **HOW** you are invested, and **WHAT** the next step is to further your investment is as real to us as is the picture of Martin Luther King delivering his dream speech; we know what is.

DANGER AT THE POINT OF JUNCTURE

The story of my visit to Tibet highlights an important aspect of achieving personal success, which may become even more important in the near future: the urgency of taking action.

Sadly, experiencing a spiritual Tibet without highways, malls, and hotels with pools, bars, and discos wasn't my only travel adventure that can't be repeated anymore.

A year later, in 1988, I traveled to Kashmir and Ladakh, also known as "Heaven on Earth" in the Indian Himalayas. Just like visiting Tibet, it was a breathtakingly beautiful, spiritual experience. But the peace didn't last. Already, the following year, conflicts erupted, which are still ongoing.

Today, streets in the capital Srinagar are locked off by roadblocks and hundreds of paramilitary troopers patrol the city and the state's main highways. In August 2019, the Indian government removed Kashmir's special autonomous status and placed the region under severe lockdown and a total communications blackout. It might be only a matter of time until things escalate even further.

Traveling to Tibet and China, I also visited Hong-Kong which, at the time, was still a British Colony. I fell so hard in love with this magnificent city that I wanted to move there. Today, Hong-Kong too is in political turmoil; the city's (relative) political freedom hangs in the balance. Watching news footage of violent demonstrations, I don't recognize the city I loved anymore.

Beyond the effects of engineering achievements (such as the Qinghai–Tibet railway) as well as political and economic developments, even environmental changes affect the plans we make for how we want to live.

Climate change is real and communities around the world struggle with it. Many agree that we are living through a crisis, even in the United States. In other parts of the world, glaciers are melting and the Amazon is burning. Every day people are waking up to the news that an environmental disaster is happening somewhere. It's a real crisis.

*

Here is an interesting fact: In the Chinese language, the word "crisis" is composed of the two Chinese characters meaning "danger at a point of juncture" and "opportunity" (traditional Chinese: 危機).

Though our parents' goals and even some of our goals of younger years may no longer be achievable, recognizing that we are living through "danger at a point of juncture" as well as "opportunities" can help us find solutions and even "reach the dream" relatively easily – if we act.

OPPORTUNITIES

As laid out in this book, for something to be "a dream," it has to BIG, really BIG, and it has to **benefit others**. Consequently, stabilizing the planet's climate is a dream because it's a collective dream-goal and it will benefit billions of people worldwide.

Which is why hundreds of thousands of people are working on ideas that join environmental and economic goals. They want to be part of achieving this dream, and they see opportunities.

For example, in 2011, Param Jaggi, a 17-year-old high school student from Plano, Texas, invented his "Algae Mobile," a device that fits over a car's tailpipe and converts the car's CO_2 emissions into oxygen while driving. For this achievement, he was awarded the EPA's sustainability award.

The same year Egyptian teenager Azza Abdel Hamid Faiad won the European Fusion Development Agreement Award at the 23rd EU Contest for Young Scientists for inventing a method to generate biofuel by breaking down plastics.

And sixteen year-old Swedish climate activist Greta Thunberg got invited to speak at the 2018 UN Climate Change Conference and the 2019 World Economic Forum in Davos. She was also featured on the cover of Time magazine, which named her a "next generation leader."

Inventing new devices or becoming an activist aren't the only opportunities. Stabilizing the planet's climate is such a huge dream that it allows **entrepreneurs from all fields** to reach immense success while working toward achieving the Uber-dream – saving the planet.

University of Berkley students Nikhil Arora and Alejandro Velez saw a major opportunity when they learned that mushrooms could be grown in coffee grounds. The two budding entrepreneurs searched for baristas who were willing to supply them coffee grounds for free and founded their company *Back to the Roots*. The company started out producing a line of organic gardening kits and soon partnered with some of the biggest companies in the United States, like Target, Costco, Walmart, Home Depot, and Nature's Path. Even more impressive, starting 2017, thousands of New York's schools began serving Back to the Roots' organic cereal to NYC students. The relatively young company displaced Kellogg, a S&P 500 company.

And who hasn't heard of LimeBike, the company that produces ride-share electric scooters and electric-assist bikes? Founded in January 2017 by Toby Sun and Brad Bao, the company was valued at 225 million dollars by October of the same year.

Even the United States' Death Care Industry recognized the trend and many undertakers began offering "green burials" which abstain from using embalming, expensive wood and metal coffins, wreaths and cut flowers, and avoiding the higher carbon footprint of cremation. This concept is really easy to "sell" to people who are concerned about the environment. Placing a metal box and embalming chemicals into the ground is not only somewhat hazardous to the environment, it's also considerably more expensive. Indeed, today, consumers are searching for undertakers who offer "green burials."

Do you think these are extreme examples? If so, please consider that the fast-food chains Burger King and Subway began offering plant-based meats, "The Impossible Burger" and the "Beyond Meatball Marinara Sub," which was also unthinkable only a decade ago.

REACHING YOUR GOAL

Today's young entrepreneurs start businesses that revolve around a cleaner environment, recycling, and everything that goes with it because they are **invested in their future**. If the icecaps melt and the Amazon delivers less oxygen, their lives will be considerably more difficult. For the same reason, the next generations will also be eco-friendly businesses' best customers. Manufacturers of "green products" don't have to explain to these consumers why they should buy green products – they already know.

Therefore anybody who wants to "gamble on success" will realize that catering to eco-conscious consumers looks much more promising than continuing "the old ways" – trying to produce and sell products cheaper than others.

In March 2019, 1.4 million students from around the world participated in the Global Climate Strike for the Future. The majority of them don't earn money and don't own credit cards – yet. Add them to the millions of millennials who already choose sustainable offerings even if they are more expensive and you can see that it's not going to be long before "greenies" will drive the U.S. economy.

Even today, North America's millennials command an anticipated spending power of approximately US $2.8 trillion dollars.

*

Sixty years ago, Americans aimed to reach a different dream which boosted the economy immensely. With the Cold War going on and the Russians launching the world's first artificial satellite Sputnik 1 (1957), Americans were wondering if the Russians were capable of delivering nuclear warheads into U.S. air space.

Hence, when the United States' charismatic young president John F.

Kennedy set a national goal of "landing a man on the Moon by the end of this decade and returning him safely to the Earth (1961)" Americans bought into the idea that achieving this dream was possible. Not even the assassination of the president could derail efforts to reach this dream.

At its peak, the Apollo program employed 400,000 people and received assistance from over 20,000 industrial firms and universities. Still, scientists weren't the only ones who focused on the Space Race.

Architects, industrial, commercial and interior designers, advertising agents, and artists added a "touch of space" to their products thereby winning new customers. Some examples of Space Age design are still standing; for example, LAX's Theme Building, which looks like a flying saucer that landed on its four feet.

Space Age design was everywhere. Small kitchen appliances like blenders and stand mixers were rocket-shaped. Most cars of the era had fins accented with rocket-like taillights. Even children's playgrounds featured climbing towers that looked like rocket ships and radar stations. And guess what TV program kept American children entertained? "The Jetsons," Hanna-Barbera's Space Age counterpart to "The Flintstones."

Reaching the dream of saving the planet will generate even more opportunities. Not only may we have to reinvent thousands of products, entrepreneurs who find ways to recycle "that old stuff," from coffee grounds to building materials, are bound to become extremely successful.

*

Even better, when trying to reach the dream to save the planet, it is almost impossible to fail. Though not all entrepreneurs will be immensely successful and/or famous, all of them will become part of something greater and have the kind of experiences that make biographies better stories.

Just like the people who marched with Martin Luther King know that they helped change the future, even though they themselves did not hold a speech on the steps of the Lincoln Memorial, people who work on stabilizing the climate know that they are changing the lives of their children and children's children for the better.

One hundred years from now, their grandchildren will still talk about them and how their grandfathers and grandmothers saw opportunities to change a problem "because it was there," thereby pushing the human race forward and achieving "the Uber-dream" of saving the planet.

There are, of course, those who think it is the world's governments' job or maybe big corporations' to fix the environment but why would anybody who wants to "reach the dream" leave an opportunity like this on the table?

Thus, if you want to improve your odds of becoming "insanely successful" but don't have a clear, defined plan like becoming an actor, a violinist, or a doctor, consider if your goal can be aligned with the Uber-dream of "saving the planet."

Then:

1. Forget about the dream (as J.K. Rowling didn't dream of a 25 billion dollar franchise when she wrote "Harry Potter"),
2. Forgive everybody you need to forgive,
3. Dig deep to find your special know-how (just like César Ritz),
4. Set a first, manageable goal (just like Mark Zuckerberg),
5. Get invested and work toward reaching that goal with all your might (just like Andy)
6. And, when you achieved that first goal and are fully invested, pick a second goal.

7. Repeat steps 5 and 6 until your personal dream begins to take shape.

The light is green! All of us are invested in our children's and childrens' children future.

ADDENDUM 1

THE 3 EVENTS THAT CAUSED A MASSIVE MINDSHIFT

1 –Eleven billion tons of surface ice melted in Greenland in one day

On August 2, 2019 the world awoke to the news that the day before, on August 1, the global sea-level rose by 0.5mm due to 11 billion tons of surface ice melting in Greenland in one day. Considering that 70 percent of the Earth's surface is covered by water this is indeed frightening.

2 – the Amazon rainforest wildfires

On August 11, 2019 environmentalists drew attention to an increase of the wave of **wildfires in the Amazon rainforest** and declared a state of emergency. It went viral almost immediately. Scientists and climate activists pointed out that the Brazilian rainforest may already be nearing a tipping point, at which the tropical rainforest cannot re-grow.

3 - Hurricane Dorian (August 24-September 10, 2019)

On August 24, 2019 Hurricane Dorian formed and quickly became the strongest hurricane detected outside the main development region MDR, the tropical Atlantic Ocean and Caribbean Sea. Dorian made landfall on Great Abaco Island in the Bahamas, with sustained winds of 185 mph, wind gusts over 220 mph, and a central barometric pressure of 911 millibar, on September 1.

On a personal note: Having lived in South Florida for sixteen years I cannot even fathom the thought of what would have happened had a hurricane of this intensity hit Miami, Florida with over 300 high-rises, 80 of which stand taller than 400 feet, and tens of thousands of boats and yachts sitting in marinas and private homes' driveways. Though I know that Florida's building code requires that skyscrapers are built to withstand hurricanes, I wonder if they'd withstand a three-day pounding by sustained winds of 185 mph and wind gusts over 220 mph.

*

Clearly, after environmentalists have been warning about the world having to face these problems for decades, we now experience "danger at a point of juncture" and people are seeing it.

A September 2019 poll conducted by the Washington Post and the Kaiser Family Foundation revealed that, in opposition to the current U.S. administration's view, 38% of Americans believe that climate change is a crisis, 38% believe it's a major problem but not a crisis, 15% think it's a minor problem and only 8% believe climate change is not a problem at all. That's almost 8 in 10 Americans who see a major problem.

RADICAL CHANGES

Whenever societies experience a mindshift massive needs arise. Two recent such moments came when Americans realized: "I need to learn how to use a computer. If I don't I'll fall behind" and "Online shopping is a real thing."

Both of these recognitions created huge opportunities for manufacturers of personal computers, programmers, website designers, ecommerce experts, educators, banks, transportation businesses, journalists and bloggers, small business owners, and even restaurant and coffee house owners whose shops are in close proximity to the offices of computer related businesses.

*

For those who are willing to do the work or who are willing to invest in "the new thing" a mindshift moment can become an express lane to success.

Remember Mark Twain's quote, "Twenty years from now you will be more disappointed by the things that you didn't do than by the ones you did do... "?

- Twenty years ago Amazon's stock price was $70 and investors could "get in" easily. Today, it's $1,823.

- Though Google was founded in 1998, its stock went public only fifteen years ago. At the time, the stock was auctioned off at $80. Today Alphabet Inc. (GOOG) closed at $1,241.

- And, in the eighties, absolutely everybody who studied computer sciences could pick and choose among job offers even if they didn't graduate from the MIT.

*

Of course, the trick in all of this is to figure out that a mindshift is happening and "get on board" as timely as possible. Which equates to "gambling on success."

(Sometimes, we err. Supposedly, Jack Nicholson, Warren Beatty, Robert Redford, Ryan O'Neal, and Dustin Hoffman turned down the role of Michael Corleone in "Godfather." Instead, barely known Al Pacino made it his break-through role and was rewarded with a first Oscar nomination.)

Then again, noticing that a new mindshift-moment with regards to protecting our environment has arrived is relatively easy. Everybody over the age of thirty has a memory of a very different climate during their childhood days. In the fifties Americans had far less proof of what the Russians were doing and whether they were capable of delivering nuclear warheads into U.S. air space or not.

*

When I listen to today's climate debate, I often hear people say,

"The government needs to do more, it's their fault, they didn't reign in the fossil fuel industry." Often these arguments are countered by the opposite point-of-view, "No, corporations need to do it. Our government is incompetent." Least often, I hear anybody say, "I see opportunities for myself. I am working on this and that."

But, working on climate change solutions could be key to reaching mind-boggling success. Though running a start-up is never easy, running a "green start-up" has major advantages – entrepreneurs don't need to run surveys to know who their potential customers are, what they want, and where to find them. The cheapest form of marketing would require no more than handing out business cards (like Coss Marte did) at environmental events.

To save the planet we'll need more:
- Activists and fact checkers – who hold our governments accountable,

- Angel investors – who provide capital for business start-ups,

- App designers and computer whizzes – who streamline processes,

- Artists – who tell the stories of what happened and give hope to the rest of us,

- Bankers – who specialize in environmental loans,

- Culinary Arts Experts – who help to avoid food waste,

- Educators – who teach best practices how to save our environment,

- Farmers – who find best ways to grow food,

- Inventors and innovators – who come up with solutions to complex problems,

- Lawyers – who specialize in environmental law,

- Media people – who share the news, good and bad,

- Packaging experts – who find better solutions than wrapping everything in plastic,

- Politicians – who create responsible laws,

- Recyclers – who help us to turn trash into treasure,

- Scientists – who do what scientists do, and even

- Writers – who specialize in the genre "environmental crimes."

Of course, this is a very incomplete list which is only meant to make a point at that there is room for every professional to make their mark; in fact, we might even have to invent new jobs.

*

Lastly – to get started you don't have to drop everything you are doing but can develop and fine tune your ideas while running a side gig. Martha Stewart started her empire out of a kitchen in her basement.

Basically, every housewife who has a talent for reviving or reworking old clothes could start a green business. The same goes for men (and women) who enjoy turning old furniture into something new. Both of these tasks are a form of recycling, the new products can be sold at local markets and/or in Internet stores.

High school students and college students can start a tree planting business in their neighborhood. And, while they are at it, maybe they'll find out that their customers have "trash that can be turned into treasure" in their garages and would even pay for having it removed.

Summing it up – Everybody can become a "green entrepreneur. "

ADDENDUM 2

It's always been my philosophy that to be effective nonfiction books should get to the point and stay on target; unnecessary fluff only distracts. Still, throughout "Naked Eye-Opener" I mentioned some of my journeys, which, even with all the money in the world, cannot be repeated anymore. Which might warrant that I offer these stories here.

If you don't like to read unusual travel adventure stories please flip to Addendum 3 "USEFUL WEBSITES" (page 106)

(Previously published in my motivational storybook memoir "Naked Determination: 41 Stories About Overcoming Fear," in 2012)

IS TIMING OF THE ESSENCE?

Inspired by the many travel and adventure books I read I decided pretty early on that I didn't need a walk-in closet full of clothes, a spacious apartment, or a sharp-looking car to be happy; my big goal in life was to travel. Ideally, I wanted to try to see the whole world. Since, at the time, I lived in Vienna in the center of Europe, most European destinations were just a train ride away.

Once I had seen most of Europe I wanted to visit the legendary destinations all travelers talked about with that certain timbre of respect. One of them was Tibet, "The Roof of the World."

At the age of eleven, I had met Heinrich Harrer, the former tutor of the Dalai Lama and author of *Seven Years in Tibet*, when he toured Austria with his book. At his lecture I had seen slides of a beautiful, vast, and wild country with a religion and spirituality I did not understand, but which seemed incredibly profound. I got to shake Harrer's hand and he signed my copy of his book. Then, he asked me if I was going to visit Tibet some day. Even though I was quite young I felt that replying "no" was not an option.

"Hurry up," the great man replied, "the Chinese are going to change Tibet."

To be sure, visiting Tibet was not an easy task. Flying there was quite costly and there was no guarantee that I'd make it to Lhasa. Since 1965 when Tibet became an autonomous province of China the Chinese government controlled who was allowed to enter Tibet and when. I had heard of travelers who even had plane tickets to Lhasa but their flights were cancelled, their money returned, and that was the end of their adventure. By 1979, when the Chinese first allowed foreigners to travel to Lhasa, only 1,200 "strangers" had ever seen the city.

Finally, in fall 1986 an opportunity came up to go on a six week vacation from shortly before Christmas till the end of January 1987. It was a bit of a scary thought to stay away from home so long. At the time, I was working as a movie production manager, I was a freelancer. In a worst case scenario, I'd come back from Asia and not have a job for weeks in a row. Pondering my options I recalled how my dad used to say, "the light doesn't get any greener," every time he saw a driver not starting to drive when the traffic light turned green. Right then, my situation looked as good as it could. I had one job lined up for March and April the following year. Though a million things could go wrong with that, clearly − "the light could not get any greener." So, I resurrected and modified an old plan to travel with the Trans-Siberian Railway through Russia to Beijing and make my way to Tibet from there.

The fact that the Chinese opened and closed Tibet at will: either allowing tourists in... or just 'not' was not the only problem. Though it seemed likely that Chinese officials wouldn't worry about a lone traveler who wanted to visit Tibet during winter, the weather could also be a factor. Tibet's capital, Lhasa, is at an elevation of 12,000 feet. Who knew if planes could make it up there, in the middle of winter.

But I was determined and started my trip on December 21, 1986, traveling exactly like I had planned – Vienna – Kiev – Moscow – Irkutsk – Harbin – Beijing – Chengdu – and then – Lhasa, Tibet.

I got lucky and absolutely everything, including the weather, worked out. The Chinese security checks were incredibly annoying but I passed and arrived at Lhasa airport on the morning of January 13, 1987.

While on the bus getting transported from the airport to the city, a trip that took more than four hours, I saw a few pilgrims prostrating themselves to their destination – their holy city. That's when it first hit me that I had arrived at a place like no other. Though I had read that Buddhist pilgrims from far away parts of the country spent years covering the entire distance body length by body length until they reached Lhasa, actually seeing the pilgrims put me in my place – I knew nothing about believing, devotion, and true faith. Here I was a beginner. Tibetans knew something I did not even know existed.

Lhasa turned out to be a mesmerizing city in a barren landscape full of breathtaking spiritual energy.

Because it was January, very few tourists arrived with me. The city itself was a slightly modernized version of Heinrich Harrer's Lhasa. Buddhism was omnipresent. There were many depictions of Buddha sitting on a lotus flower painted on rocky cliffs. Prayer flags were flying everywhere. At this altitude the air is cleaner, the light is brighter, and every impression is more intense.

Surprisingly, a most striking moment came on my first morning in Lhasa. Arriving in Tibet the day before had meant that I flew to an elevation of about 12,000 feet in only two hours. Thirty minutes later I was suffering from altitude sickness. Because there was no transportation I had to walk from the bus terminal to my hotel, carrying my 40 pounds of luggage. It took me one hour to get there and multiple stops to catch my breath.

The hotel was of rectangular shape with an outhouse with showers and toilets in the center of the courtyard. I was informed that hot showers would only be available between 8:00 and 10:00 a.m. Because I was too exhausted to make another step I did not care and took a room on the second floor. Then I slept like a baby.

Early the next morning I awoke when I heard murmurs outside my door, on the balcony. I sensed something special was going on out there, jumped out of my bed and grabbed my camera. Then I opened the door and there it was – the picture which would be burned into my memory forever. It's unbelievable beauty and symbolic character were not to be overlooked.

Like from everywhere else in town, I could see the white Potala Palace on its hill. The magnificent symbol of Buddhist religion and spirituality towered over the needy buildings in the foreground. The early morning sunrays lit up the Potala's white walls in a glowing red. Indeed it looked as if the Potala Palace itself was in flames.

Right behind the Potala stood a dark gray cloud and behind that was the ever-so-beautiful blue morning sky. I lifted my camera and clicked the button. Not a minute later the sun's rays were strong enough that the red coloring of the Potala's walls faded. Just in time I had snapped a picture which was symbolic for religion and culture in Tibet – a dark cloud was hanging over its intense and quiet beauty. To me and maybe to the Tibetans who stood next to me it felt as if Buddha himself was sending a warning sign that the Tibetans' way of life was threatened.

Because I could only stay for four days, I was determined to make the most out of my visit. That was not always easy. Comfort was nonexistent. Like most other tourists I downed aspirins as blood thinner to fight altitude sickness. I lived off dough-cakes baked on a street vendor's red-glowing cast-iron oven and Yak-butter tea. Gaining strength every day I was finally ready to walk up to the Potala where I was going to visit the Dalai Lama's private chambers.

As surprising as this may sound, I did not have any expectations. Though I had seen Harrer's black and white photographs of Tibet I had never seen the inside of the Potala, maybe because in the fifties photographic film wasn't sensitive enough to capture pictures in rooms lit by yak-butter lamps or because considerate people didn't take pictures inside places of worship.

Only half a dozen other "strangers" passed through the entrance gate with me. Within minutes we lost sight of each other inside the huge palace. In prayer rooms monks smiled friendly at me but I sensed they were in another world and we did not connect. In a way, meeting them was humbling. Even though I was that girl who could live without a walk-in closet full of clothes and be just fine, next to the humble, pious monks I felt like a vain person.

There were no guides or signs but eventually I made my way to the top floor and found the Dalai Lama's quarters quite easily. The room's aura was absolutely mesmerizing.

The windows were open and bright light filled the room. The Dalai Lama's former golden throne sparkled in the sunlight, outshining the beautiful mural in the back, not in a rich or golden way but seeming to say, "his Holiness sat right here and thought about how to help the world become a more compassionate place." And, then there were the sheer, orange curtains. The steadily blowing winds had pulled them outside where they flapped like prayer flags forming a connection to heaven. To me it appeared as if they transmitted a message, in code; I had arrived at the place where everybody could meditate with ease.

In Tibet, time seemed to be measured by the clacker of metallic prayer mills, not only for Tibetans but also for travelers like me. I wandered through the Jokhang Temple where I studied the faces of incredibly peaceful statues of Buddha, visited the market place to watch the people do their bidding and trading, and went down to the river where I sat on the bridge and waited for more pilgrims to arrive. The only place where I'd meet foreigners was the British Tea House, which had been set up or built by the British but wasn't British in any way at all. By the time I had to leave I was certain that I would return. In fact, I had big plans. If I could manage to take a two to three months vacation I'd return. Maybe I could even cross the Gampala pass and make it to Shigatse, Tibet.

The last leg of my journey led me to Hong-Kong from where I planned to fly back to Europe. The difference between Tibet's bare vulnerability and Hong Kong's pulsating life as a center for finance and business could not have not have been any greater. Seeing Hong-Kong I could guess what power China would develop into in 1997, when it would resume sovereignty of this city. I was certain that China would not change Hong-Kong, but use it as a door to the West.

China's GDP would keep growing and in 2006, nine years after China took back Hong-Kong, the Qinghai–Tibet Railway would be opened. Like visionary concepts often do, the railroad changed everything. Goods could now be brought easily into Tibet. In addition to that, trains are equipped with two oxygen supply systems which allow tourists to avoid issues with altitude sickness.

What was an incredible adventure two decades earlier was now a train trip away. Just like Mt. Everest 280 miles to the west-south-west, Lhasa had become a business opportunity.

Update:

In 1986, 22,000 tourists, an average of 60 tourists per day, visited

91

Tibet (though not during winter), and in 2018, 30 million tourists visited Tibet (not Lhasa), which equates to an average of 80,000 visitors per day.

WHAT DO WE REALLY NEED?
(Penned in 2012)

Traveling was an expensive hobby, even though I never went on a single luxury trip. In fact, I always traveled as cheap as possible. I have slept in youth hostels and tents, on trains and benches in train stations, and even in a lifeboat once or twice.

To feed my hobby I never purchased anything I didn't really need. Even when working in the movie industry, getting paid a great salary for working 60+ hours per week, eating for free on the set, and getting paid mileage for commuting to and from work, I lived in a tiny 400 square feet apartment and drove a 10-year old VW Rabbit, so tiny that I could have parked it sideways into a U.S. parking space. I dressed almost exclusively in jeans and T-shirts and hardly ever ate out. I never went to sporting events, did not own a TV, and rarely ever shopped for anything but food. But, I traveled – on average to two to three countries per year.

One of my must-see destinations was the Kashmir region. North of Pakistan and India and bordered by China in the East, that region is involved in a boundary dispute between these three countries. There have been continuous conflicts since 1947 but I wanted to travel there because the region has some of the most beautiful and dramatic landscapes on Earth.

Going there involved an additional, unusual challenge. Though I never traveled with groups because I wanted to be flexible and also didn't want to pay tour guides' fees, there was no way of avoiding it when visiting Ladakh, the eastern region of Kashmir. Ladakh is known as the *Land of Passes* and difficult to travel. Since the only way how goods (including cars) could be brought in and out of the valley led across unpaved high-altitude roads few rental jeeps were available and leased exclusively to tourist groups. Hence it took till 1988 until I found a travel agency that offered adventure trips to the locations I wanted to see.

I would fly to Srinagar, the capital of Jammu and Kashmir, famous for its houseboats on Dal Lake. To be precise, for a few days I was going to live on a houseboat.

From there I would travel via bus to Kargil and Padum in the Zanskar Valley. Zanskar Valley, also called *The Virgin Valley*, was and maybe still is the most isolated of the valleys in the Indian Himalayas. Next, the journey would lead back to Kargil and then via jeep to Leh, the historical capital of Ladakh and once a major crossroad on the ancient Silk Route.

*

Starting our road trip in Srinagar it became clear that Ladakh and Zanskar were special worlds. They had to be conquered, almost in the literal sense of the word. To get there we had to cross the Zoji-La (Pass) at an elevation of 11,575 feet. With Srinagar's elevation being 5,200 feet we needed to climb more than 5,000 feet on a road which was mostly unpaved and single lane.

Since the road could be traveled only one way, traffic was exclusively going up or down for hours. We had to wait in line with about 200 other vehicles – buses, military trucks, and shoddy sedans. Guards watched that nobody snuck by the gate arm. They also informed us that if any of the vehicles broke down we could be stuck on the pass for up to half a day. Finally the barrier opened and our bus began moving up the pass with the caravan of other vehicles.

The Zoji-La was a challenge even for seasoned drivers. There were no guardrails and no room for error. Most often the road was barely wider than the trucks and buses; with a rocky cliff rising on one side and a steep, nearly vertical, cliff falling straight down on the other. The only places where the road widened at all were in the hairpin bends. Never minding the steep gradient some drivers tried to bypass other vehicles in these road curves. Saying I feared for my life would be too much but it was the most adventurous ride of my life. Still we got up the pass relatively easily. It would not be the same going back.

Having arrived we admired mountain ranges with peaks of more than 17,000 feet and their glaciers, trekked to monasteries, where we learned about Buddhism, and also spotted the rare Blue Poppy

(Meconopsis betonicifolia). All the while we camped – though in style. We had a team of drivers, cooks, and helpers, who handled all related tasks. The main reason for this effort was that there was no infrastructure to support our small troop of travelers. Even our food had to be brought in on its own supply truck.

After busy days of cherishing breathtaking sights there were the evenings. Luckily, I was traveling with like minded people. All of us were bitten by the same travel bug. Sitting together in our tent camp we told each other travel stories and discussed what other destinations we absolutely had to see.

Before we retreated into our sleeping bags we always took at least fifteen minutes to admire the starry sky in its enormity. It was a view visible only at these elevations. Up there was no air pollution and not even a hint of foggy residue obstructed our view of the stars. I could not help but feeling like a navigator of the olden days might have felt standing on the bridge of a caravel and reading the night sky. Every day, we fell asleep knowing that right there and then nothing else mattered. If the Dow-Jones Index would have dropped by 1,000 points we would not have heard about it and even if we did this would still have been the most beautiful night sky – grand, eternal, and completely peaceful.

It was equally amazing to wake up in this setting. I had a tiny alarm clock which I put in my shirt pocket so I could turn it off after the first beep. Every day I set it so it'd wake up before dawn. Then, I sat in front of the tent and watched the sun coming up in a valley in between the peaks. If I'd have to describe one picture that symbolizes hope and determination combined in one image it'd be that sight.

I had been fascinated with the Himalayas and their people since I had traveled to Tibet the previous year. There is something incredibly majestic about mountains which seem to scratch the perfectly blue sky with their white peaks. The contours of everything the sun shines at are so much sharper and at night the stars not only seemed closer, we were in fact about 11,000 feet closer.

But nothing had prepared me for meeting Ladakhi and Zanskari people. Since tourists could not fly to the valleys and crossing the Zoji-La was almost an expedition there was extremely little Western influence. The valleys were the first region I traveled to where I could not spot a single one of the famous red soda cans. Considering how difficult it was to bring materials up the pass plus the Zoji-La pass being mostly closed during the six months of winter obviously nobody bothered to move any unnecessary stuff up the pass.

Almost all Kashmiri and Zanskari people we met wore their traditional garbs. Many children were barefoot though they wore woven wool hats. Most surprisingly I did not see anybody wearing sunglasses. Whereas in Tibet I saw plenty of market stands selling sunglasses there weren't any in Kashmir and Zanskar. Considering the glare of the August sun that was remarkable. It was the absence of something which I felt was an absolute necessity. Never having been a dresser I felt weird even about wearing my great pair of trekking shoes. Of course I had purchased the shoes thinking that it was the bare minimum I needed, but the people, who lived in the valleys, did fine without.

We trekked to three monasteries where I could not stop myself from observing the monks. They appeared to be happy at all times and I had to study their faces closely to spot only one monk who wasn't smiling.

On our trekking adventures we also saw many locals bringing in grains. Women carried huge bales, typically two by three feet, and three feet high. It looked like backbreaking work but they too appeared to be happy. There were also quite a few teenagers, girls and boys, who carried some kind of green plants in round wooden baskets of about two feet in diameter. I wondered what these teenagers were thinking when they saw us. Many of my fellow travelers had obviously expensive gear. I had at least really cool shoes. The Kashmiris didn't even have sunglasses.

It was easy to imagine that the Kashmiri people felt at least a bit of envy. But if there was some I did not see it. They just smiled at us and seemed happy in a way European and American people aren't ever happy. I sensed a certain curiosity but it did not feel like wanting to have something of what we had. I couldn't help but wondering if my European friends and their children wanted to know what all Kashmiris seemed to know – real happiness that wasn't tied to any material possessions.

*

While we were in Kashmir the president of Pakistan, Muhammad Zia-Ul-Haq, died in a plane crash. From our drivers we learned that many Pakistanis didn't believe that this was an accident but that India had shot down the plane. Conditions became a bit dicey and it was suggested that we shouldn't use the jeeps. Instead, our whole group of twenty-eight people had to travel from Leh to Kargil standing in an open truck which obviously had been used to transport animals. We could smell it.

Traveling over bad roads while standing on the back of a truck can only be described as brain rattling. Travel time seemed to double up. Back on the bus and traveling down Zoji-La we got stuck behind another bus, which had collided with a road construction vehicle and so we got stuck on Zoji-La. For a while it almost felt as if the valleys wouldn't let us leave.

Eventually we made it back to Srinagar. Sitting on the top deck of our houseboat, I enjoyed tea-time the British way: Earl Grey with milk, no lemon, no sugar. I thought about the happy people up there in the mountains. Quite obviously it is not stuff that brings happiness. The way they lived was proof that real peace came from the inside. Peace was… being under that great sky, experiencing the universe. The feeling was so grand it could not be interfered with by anything. Maybe the people of Zanskar and Ladakh were so happy because they had that every day. Maybe that was why they were at ease with themselves and us, who we had things they did not have.

*

A year later, in 1989, the peace was gone. To this day it hasn't returned. As I wrote this book I wondered why it was that I got lucky to experience what I was looking for again and again – just in time. Then again, I didn't believe in waiting to get lucky. I was actively looking for opportunities and when they came up I didn't wait but directed all my energies toward accomplishing my goals.

IS OUR BLUE PLANET'S COLOR FADING?
(Penned in 2012)

In late October 1982, on my first trans-Atlantic flight to New York, aboard Alia, the Royal Jordanian Airline, I got to sit next to an Arabic, presumably Jordanian, gentleman. Well-dressed, well-groomed, and well-build he looked like a business man ready to make some fabulous deal in America. As the plane took off he introduced himself and very politely tried to start a conversation. I was impressed with his manners and efforts but did not know how to handle the conversation. His English skills were so rudimentary I had to ask clarifying questions nonstop. I thought doing that might make me look terribly impolite and rude.

"So, what will you be doing in New York," I continued our ongoing conversation, "Business or sight-seeing?"

"Oh," he said, "I go back to Jordan."

"Yes," I said and smiled, "But in between? What will you be doing *whiiile* in New York?"

"I go back."

This was frustrating. He did not seem to understand what I was asking. I took a new approach.

"How many days will you stay in New York?"

"I go back tomorrow."

"TOMORROW??? Why are you even going to New York?"

Hearing his unexpected answer I became determined to find out what his trip was all about. I offered a new angle: "New York is a great city with lots of great things to do!"

The "businessman" smiled briefly and said in a most neutral tone, "I go back because I guard the plane."

Now I got insecure. Was this guy trying to pull one on me? I decided to play along.

"Oh," I said and giggled, "You are a security officer?"

"YES!" he said, apparently relieved that I had uttered the right word.

Of course I did not believe him. I thought he wanted to impress me but I wasn't going to let him get away with his little charade.

"Really?" I said, and then, teasing him, "So, surely you have a gun?"

"Yes," the Arab gentleman said, smiling politely. He must have realized that I did not believe a word of what he was saying. After a brief pause he pulled up one knee so it almost reached his chin and pulled up his trouser to reveal a huge gun strapped to the inside of his lower leg, covering almost the entire length of it.

I gasped. I had never seen one of those things up close. Now I certainly felt protected. I also did not know what to say. Really, what is the appropriate response in such a situation? This man had to be a sky marshal. I had heard about them but up to that point never even known if they really existed or if it was just a rumor to make passengers feel safe. Thank God, he did not wait for me to reply but came back with an extraordinary proposition.

"Do you wish to see the captain and the cockpit?" he asked.

"YES," I said delighted, "I would love to." (*Did I want to see the cockpit of a Boeing 747? Who wouldn't?*)

"One moment," the sky marshal said and disappeared. Five minutes later he was back and proudly announced, "In twenty minutes."

Twenty minutes later he escorted me up the staircase of the Boeing 747. We walked through the first class to the cockpit door. He knocked and the captain let us in. While the captain introduced himself and the rest of the crew, I could not help but stare by him, looking out the window. Considering how special this occasion was, I knew I was rude, very rude, but I could not help it. The view was so magical I just could not take my eyes off what I saw.

There was 'the universe'. It appeared as if we were flying right into outer space.

Contrary to any window in the aircraft cabin, the cockpit window offered a majestic, panoramic view of the universe, in movie terms it was the difference between 16mm and 70 mm widescreen.

The planet below us looked curved, yet we seemed to fly in a straight line – just straight out into the atmosphere. Of course I had seen tons of pictures showing the Earth as blue planet, the planet with water and livable conditions, but the real Earth just had an additional dimension that cannot be captured in any picture. Right at that moment I knew I could look at this view for hours and never grow tired of seeing it.

It was also at that moment that I became an environmentalist. What we have here on Earth is so special; we need to do everything we can to keep it that way.

*

Now, a quarter of a century later, I see a global environmental catastrophe approaching like a tsunami. Our world, the blue planet, is losing its blue color. The earth is getting dirtier, our oceans are turning into 'garbage soups,' and the Earth's atmosphere is getting more and more polluted every day. Searching for the term 'garbage patch' on YouTube is a shocking experience. Nobody fills their own home with trash, yet, collectively, we seem to fill our greater home with garbage. If our societies do not start making rapid changes, our lifestyle will make our planet an uninhabitable environment. Once this planet loses its blue color, it will just have a shade of brown... or gray... or beige... like all others.

AFTER THOUGHT

There is so much we can do! Reduce, Reuse, Recycle is only the beginning. The worldwide web is a never ending resource for solutions tailored to every budget.

Beyond that, we have the power to force entire industries to do the right thing by favoring the products which are produced in an eco-friendly way. This is a consumer driven society and therefore we are in charge!

ADDENUM 3
USEFUL WEBSITES THAT WILL STIMULATE YOUR CREATIVITY

(The author makes no claim to the accuracy or completeness of the included list of relevant articles and expressly disclaims liability for errors or omissions. This list merely meant to offer ideas to inspire readers to find their own solutions.)

2 SURVEYS

Americans increasingly see climate change as a crisis, poll shows by Brady Dennis, Steven Mufson and Scott Clement, September 13, 2019
https://www.washingtonpost.com/climate-environment/americans-increasingly-see-climate-change-as-a-crisis-poll-shows/2019/09/12/74234db0-cd2a-11e9-87fa-8501a456c003_story.html
- - - - - - -*- - - - - -

How Americans see climate change in 5 charts by Cary Funk and Brian Kennedy, September 15, 2019
https://www.pewresearch.org/fact-tank/2019/04/19/how-americans-see-climate-change-in-5-charts/
- - - - - - -*- - - - - -

ACTIVISM

If you'd like to become a climate activist you'll be in good company.
Harrison Ford | 2018 Global Climate Action Summit
https://youtu.be/99AwWQ-M2_M

- - - - - -*- - - - - -

You Are Stealing Our Future: Greta Thunberg, 15, Condemns the World's Inaction on Climate Change
https://youtu.be/HzeekxtyFOY

- - - - - -*- - - - - -

Al Roker Climate change is not ignorable. It's time to stop debating what is staring us all in our faces.
https://www.nbcnews.com/think/opinion/climate-change-not-ignorable-it-s-time-stop-debating-what-ncna1054296

- - - - - -*- - - - - -

EVENTS

Calendar of Global Environmental Events
http://www.globalstewards.org/environmental-calendar.htm

- - - - - -*- - - - - -

INNOVATION

Anthony Bourdain STARZ Documentary "WASTED! THE STORY OF FOOD WASTE" Teaser Trailer
https://youtu.be/703x_tSN4P4

- - - - - -*- - - - - -

The next food movement? Maybe garbage-to-plate dining
https://youtu.be/roNh6Rtryx4

- - - - - -*- - - - - -

106

Hemp used for construction gains popularity in U.S.
https://www.upi.com/Top_News/US/2019/07/18/Hemp-used-for-construction-gains-popularity-in-US/6831563287029/
- - - - - -*- - - - - -

7 Zero Waste Designers who Are Just Killing It
https://eluxemagazine.com/fashion/zero-waste-designers/
- - - - - -*- - - - - -

Coolest Clothing From Recycled Scraps
https://youtu.be/ihORCL36r0E
- - - - - -*- - - - - -

These T-shirts are made to be remade (Teemill)
https://www.cnn.com/videos/business/2019/09/27/circular-fashion-teemill-t-shirts-biz-evolved-lon-orig.cnn/video/playlists/stories-worth-watching/
- - - - - -*- - - - - -

The Order of the Good Death
http://www.orderofthegooddeath.com/resources/natural-burial
- - - - - -*- - - - - -

YOUNG ENTREPRENEURS

Ryan's Recycling - 9-Year-Old Entrepreneur Goes Green and then Goes Global!
https://youtu.be/h8fhuQtr70o
- - - - - -*- - - - - -

AWARDS

Environmental Awards
https://en.wikipedia.org/wiki/Category:Environmental_awards
- - - - - -*- - - - - -

SPACE AGE DESIGN

Archive Gallery: How the Space Age Influenced Design
https://www.popsci.com/technology/article/2011-06/archive-gallery-how-space-age-influenced-design/

-------*------

Atomic Age Furniture
https://tinyurl.com/y24bv399

-------*------

Sputnik Chandeliers
https://tinyurl.com/y52n6d8c

-------*------

Radar defense station in American playground
https://commons.wikimedia.org/wiki/File:Radar_defense_station_in_American_playground.jpg

-------*------

GREEN SHOPPING POWER

Green Generation: Millennials Say Sustainability Is a Shopping Priority
https://www.nielsen.com/us/en/insights/article/2015/green-generation-millennials-say-sustainability-is-a-shopping-priority/

-------*------

MONEY

Environmental Grants & Loans
https://www.sba.gov/content/environmental-grants-loans-0

-------*------

EPA Grants (U.S. Department of Environmental Protection)
https://www.epa.gov/grants

-------*------

Under the small business innovation grants two types of grants are awarded: Small Business Technology Transfer (STTR) and Small Business Innovation Research (SBIR).

Federal agencies that award the grants:
- the Environmental Protection Agencies (EPA),
- the Department of Defense,
- the Department of Energy,
- the Department of Transportation,
- the Department of Health and Human Services,
- the Department of Health of Agriculture,
- National Oceanic and Atmospheric Administration (NOAA),
- National Science Foundation
- National Institute of Standards and Technology (NIST)

- - - - - -*- - - - - -

THANK YOU for buying

NAKED EYE-OPENER
To Reach the Dream
You Must Forget About It

Please leave a review at Amazon.com – other readers care about
your opinion.

***

I hope you will find a reason to give
NAKED EYE-OPENER
To Reach the Dream You Must Forget About It
as a gift to

your child(ren),
your relatives, and
your best friends

to help them
to achieve their goals, too.

***

About the Author

I was born in Vienna, Austria, but I don't ski, yodel or play an instrument. And, even though it's one of the most famous musical drama movies, I watched the "Sound of Music" with Julie Andrews only after I found out that all my American friends had seen the movie. At least, I show off my roots by watching the Vienna New Year's Concert (Neujahrskonzert) and the famed Hahnenkamm downhill, religiously.

To be honest, I'd rather be a world-citizen. These days pretty much everything we do affects people elsewhere. I feel very fortunate to have had so many amazing experiences on my travels around the world.

Never shying away from insane work, I analyzed 100,000+ emails for effectiveness and personal appeal to devise a method to write best emails. After all, writing best emails is the most effective way to reach customers and influencers. I also dug through thousands of online reviews to find out how to get them and how they can help to boost sales. My work has been featured on Bloomberg, in SUCCESS, and in Entrepreneur.

If I have found one truth in life, then it is:

"Go for it! Do the work because it will pay off, enjoy the moment because it might not last!"

*

Gisela Hausmann is a proud mother of two and grandmother of one. She lives with her two cats, Artemis and Yin-Yang, in Greenville, SC.

Gisela Hausmann's "naked (meaning no-fluff) books"

As an author I believe that it is unreasonable to expect readers to read non-fiction books peppered with fluff.

This is my books' concept:

1) "Naked" how-to books deliver knowledge in the **shortest, most efficient and most entertaining** manner; they are supported by illustrations, which show and tell.

2) "Naked" no-fluff books energize readers, because readers do not have to labor through the pages but can **see what works and why** it works.

3) "Naked" books **empower readers** because reading no-fluff books builds up energy. Readers do not feel drained but feel energized from learning dozens of easy-to-follow strategies and solutions in a short time.

4) "Naked" is to books what **"lean"** is to business; waste information is removed; solutions and action steps are introduced.

5) **"Naked" no-fluff books are so 21st century**... Today, we do not have time to dig for solutions; we want to buy, learn, and win!

Please find more of my books at:

http://www.giselahausmann.com/books.html

Gisela Hausmann is the winner of the

- 2016 Sparky Award "Best Subject Line" (industry award)

- 2018 IAN Book of the Year Awards Finalist
- 2018 Gold Readers' Favorite Award
- 2017 IAN Book of the Year Awards Finalist
- 2016 International Book Awards Finalist
- 2016 National Indie Excellence Awards Finalist
- 2015 Kindle Book Awards Finalist
- 2014 Gold Readers' Favorite Award
- 2013 Bronze eLit Awards

To find out about upcoming 'naked books'
please subscribe at

http://www.giselahausmann.com/

Please know that this author is an email evangelist.
I value and respect subscribers and
will not inundate you with sales emails.

Hopefully, you'll connect with me

Amazon
https://www.amazon.com/Gisela-Hausmann/e/B000APN192

Twitter
https://twitter.com/Naked_Determina

Linkedin
https://www.linkedin.com/in/gisela-hausmann-03404913/

Pinterest
https://www.pinterest.com/ghausmann1856/

Web:
https://giselahausmann.com/

Blogger
https://nakeddetermination.blogspot.com/

Huffington Post
https://www.huffpost.com/author/gisela-hausmann-259

For speaking engagements please write to
mailto:gisela.hausmann@yahoo.com

*

MORE BOOKS

About writing best emails:

- NAKED WORDS 2.0: The Effective 157-Word Email
- NAKED TEXT Email Writing Skills for Teenagers
- 73 Ways to Turn a Me-Mail Into an E-mail

Biography:

- Naked Determination, 41 Stories About Overcoming Fear

Books for indie authors:
- Naked News for Indie Authors How NOT to Invest Your Marketing $$$
- BOOK MARKETING: The Funnel Factor: Including 100 Media Pitches (paperback only)
- Naked Good Reads: How to find Readers
- The Little Blue Book for Authors: 53 Dos & Don'ts Nobody Is Telling You
- The Little Blue Book for Authors: 101 Clues to Get More Out of Facebook
- The Little Blue Book for Authors: Essential Manners for the Modern Author

About Getting Online Reviews:
- NAKED TRUTHS About Getting Book Reviews 2018
- NAKED TRUTHS About Getting Book Reviews: by Amazon Top Reviewer Gisela Hausmann
- NAKED TRUTHS About Getting Product Reviews on Amazon.com: 7 Insider tips to boost Sales (paperback only)
- BAT SHIT CRAZY Review Requests: Email Humor (paperback only)

<u>Environmental fiction:</u>

- Are We Nuts?

<u>Nonfiction/Blog Books:</u>

- How I Built Myself a Hobbit Fire Pit
- NAKED ELABORATIONS: Our Time to 'Fix Things' Is Running Out

* * *

*

Notes

www.ingramcontent.com/pod-product-compliance
Lightning Source LLC
Chambersburg PA
CBHW070106070426
42448CB00038B/1830